Names for Girls and Boys . . .

ISLA (Scottish) May mean literally 'from the Isles'.

ISLEAN (Celtic. Pron: ileen) 'sweetvoiced'. Var. and dim., Isleen, Islaen, Isla.

ISMAY (Pron: ismay). A rare name used in the 13th century. Var., Ysmay, Isamaya.

ISMENIA maybe of Celtic origin. The meaning is uncertain (it is not connected to the Greek Ismene).

ISOLDA (Old German) 'ice rule'. Var., Isolde.

ISOLINE (Celtic) 'fair'.

GABOR (Hungarian) 'hero of God'.

GABRIEL (Hebrew) 'strongman of God'. Dim., Gabby, Gabe. Var., Gabryell.

GALAHAD (Welsh) The name of the knight who found the Holy Grail.

GALLEN (Greek) 'healer'.

GALLIN probably Celtic 'little stranger'.

GALVIN (Celtic) 'the sparrow'. Dim., Vin, Vinny.

Compiled by

CAROLE BOYER

Names for Girls and Boys

GRANADA

London Toronto Sydney New York

Published by Granada Publishing Limited in 1974
Reprinted 1976, 1977, 1979 (twice), 1980, 1981 (twice), 1982, 1983

ISBN 0 583 12390 2

Originally published in two volumes
titled *Names for Girls* and *Names for Boys*
by Mayflower Books in Compact form
Copyright © Mayflower Books 1970

Granada Publishing Limited
Frogmore, St Albans, Herts AL2 2NF
and
36 Golden Square, London W1R 4AH
515 Madison Avenue, New York, NY 10022, USA
117 York Street, Sydney, NSW 2000, Australia
60 International Blvd, Rexdale, Ontario, R9W 6J2, Canada
61 Beach Road, Auckland, New Zealand

Made and printed in Great Britain by
Richard Clay (The Chaucer Press) Ltd
Bungay, Suffolk
Set in Monotype Times

Granada ®
Granada Publishing ®

INTRODUCTION

Names have always been difficult to choose because of the great importance we attach to them. Our names become linked to our individuality like labels for the personality. When we think of a noun, such as 'table' it may bring to mind all sorts of tables, but when we think of a person's name we think exclusively of him. Long ago children were given names commemorating the manner of their birth – such as Jacob, 'taken by the heel', or Agrippa, 'born with feet foremost'; names that celebrated some distinctive facet of their personal appearance – Aurelius, 'the golden haired', or Edom, 'red'. Sometimes they were named in a hopeful manner anticipating qualities or skills the parents thought desirable. They were given bird or animal names, such as Jonah, Columba, Golubica, 'the dove'. They were given the names of weapons, as Hildebrand, 'the battle sword'. Religious names were given to them like Jedidiah, 'loved of God'. They named them also after precious stones, flowers, or anything remarkable or beautiful. But even in ancient times the meaning of a name had often become obscure by the time its use had become general, so people carried on the use of names they liked the sound of.

A Christian name is a tricky thing. It is subject to irreverent criticism from children at school. It can become shortened in an uncomplimentary fashion, or into a sound bearing little resemblance to its original (as Peggy for Margaret). Bound for life to its surname it may yet clash with it unmercifully, as in Lew Cheney, Catherine Katz could turn against its owner in the form of Kittie. Mellifluous Italian names like Alfonso, or Orsino, might seem in ten years time a little fanciful attached to one born without foreign connections in the British Isles. Some names are immediately pleasing; 'yes, definitely, I like that'. But then doubt may set in, 'It's not a name I've heard before, are there people called by that?' This is probably one of the reasons for the influence of films and television on the naming of children; the film star is evidence that the name exists.

The euphony of names is caused by the same letters occurring in the Christian name as in the surname, or by letters giving the same length of sound; like Inigo Jones, with its two o's and its two n's, or Robert Bruce, with its two b's. Ethelred the Unready was not a particularly great man, but the name he was given lingers on; partly because it's funny, but also because of the extraordinary number of its complimentary sounds. (Eh-eh red, red. The 'th' sound of Ethelred goes with the 'the', the 'y' of Unready also goes with the 'ee' sound of the 'the'. All the vowels except for the matching 'y' and 'e', are short; Oonready would spoil it as much for sound as it would for sense.) Roughly speaking every time you get a vowel you get a syllable. Christian names with two or three syllables often go well with surnames which have only one, like Sandie Shaw, Cassius Clay, or Lena Horne. Or the other way round, Joan Crawford, Charles Dickens, Anna Pavlova. John Stewart Mill is a name which has no matching sounds in it but the uneven distribution of syllables makes it a distinctive name. On the other hand if both names begin with the same letter, it can sound self-conscious or slightly comic, as Billy Bunter, Burlington Bertie, Jevan Jackson, or Clara Cluck.

Faced with a welter of names judgement soon begins to fade, but if a name pleases you when you first hear it, it will probably continue to do so. Finally, there is no true guide but your own liking, and though among the following there may be many names you will not like – others perhaps you will – *Carole Boyer*

Among the sources and works of reference I have consulted were the following:

E. M. Withycomb: Oxford Dictionary of English Christian names; Charlotte M. Yonge: History of Christian Names; The Works of Shakespeare; The Works of G. B. Shaw; The Works of W. B. Yeats; Pan Book of Boys' Names; The Bible; Hampstead and Camden (electoral) registers; Cornish (electoral) registers; Scottish (electoral) registers; Midland (electoral) registers; The Book of Saints compiled by The Benedictine Monks of St. Augustine's Abbey, Ramsgate; Parish registers of England, Cox; Robert Graves: Greek Myths; F. E. Halliday: Richard Carew of Anthony.

I am also indebted to J. Alcorn for her knowledge of phonetics.
                                                                    C.B.

Names which might leave some question as to their pronunciation have been given an imitative guide to their sound. For example – the name George would be written in imitated pronunciation as – Jawj.

The following list gives:

(a)   The sound as it is spoken
(b)   A name in which it is found
(c)   The name as it is written in imitated pronunciation.

(a)	(b)	(c)
			u	Sutton	sutton
			o	Osric	osrik
aw	Vaughan	vawn	o	Lomax	lomax
a	Pat	pat	oo	Bruce	broos
ah	Arthur	ahther	yu	Ulysses	yuliseez
ay	Stacy	staysi	g	Gershwin	gersh-win
e	Leonard	lenard			
ee	Caesar	seezer	j	George	jawj
i	Inigo	inigo	k	Callum	kalum
i	Ivor	ivaer	s	Cecil	sesil

NAMES FOR GIRLS

A

ABELLONA (Greek. Pron: abelona) 'of Apollo'. Var., Apollonia.

ABIGAIL (Hebrew) 'source of joy'. Var. and dim., Abagail Ab, Abbe, Abbi, Abby, Gael, Gail, Gale, Gayl.

ACCALIA (Latin) 'one who instigates things'. Var. and dim., Acalia, Calia, Calie.

ACIMA (Hebrew. Pron: assima) 'the Lord will judge'.

ADA (Old German. Pron: ayda) 'joyous', or 'prosperous'. Var. and dim., Aida, Eda, Adda, Ad, Addie, Addy.

ADAH (Hebrew. Pron: aydah) 'ornament'. See also **ADAIHA**.

ADAIHA (Hebrew. Pron: aydai) 'the adorned of God'. Var. and dim., Adaha, Adah, Aiha.

ADAMINA (Hebrew) 'red earth'. Var. and dim., Adamanah, Adamanna, Adaminah, Adama.

ADELA, ADELE (Old German) 'noble cheer'.

ADELAIDE (Old German) 'noble and of kind spirit'. Var. and dim., Adalia, Adaline, Adela, Adele, Adelia, Adelina, Adelind, Adeline, Adella, Adia, Dela, Della; plus all var. and dim. of **ADA**.

ADELINE another name derived from the Old German 'noble'. Introduced to England by the Norman Conquest.

ADIEL (Hebrew) 'ornament of the Lord'. Var. and dim., Addiel, Adiell, Ad, Addi, Addie, Addy.

ADONCIA (Latin) 'sweet'. Pron: adonsia.

ADRIENNE (Latin) 'woman of the sea'. Feminine of Adrian. Var., Adria, Adriana, Adriane, Adrianna, Adrianne.

AEMILIANA (Latin. Pron: amiliyana) 'industrious'.

AGATHA (Greek) 'good'. Var. and dim., Agathe, Agathy, Ag, Aggie, Aggy.

AGEE (Hebrew. Pron: ajee) 'one who flees'. Var. and dim., Agae, Agre, Aggi.

AGLAIA (Latin. Pron: aglaya) 'brightness'.

AGNES (Greek) 'pure, chaste; gentle'. Var. and dim., Agna, Agnella, Nessie, Nesta, Neysa, Annis, Amnys, Anneyce, Anese, Tagget, Agnyta.

AIA (Hebrew. Pron: aya) 'wife'.

AIDA see **ADA**.

AILEEN either the Irish equivalent of Helen or of the Old German Avelina, introduced into the British Isles by the Normans. Var., Alene, Aline, Eileen, Iline, Illene.

AILSA (Old German. Pron: aylsa) 'girl of cheer'. Var. and dim., Aillsa, Ailssa, Ilsa.

AIMEE (French. Pron: aymay) 'loved'.

AKILINA (Latin) 'eagle'. Dim., Lina.

ALANA (Celtic) 'handsome or fair'. Feminine of Alan. Var. and dim., Alana, Allana, Alina, Lana, Lane.

ALARICE (Old German. Pron: alaris) 'ruler of all'. Feminine of Alaric. Var., Alarise.

ALBERTA (Old German) 'noble and brilliant'. Feminine of Albert. Var. and dim., Albertina, Albertine, Elberta, Bert, Berta, Berte, Bartie.

ALBINIA (Latin) 'white'. Var., Albina.

ALDA (Old German) 'rich'.

ALDIS (Old English. Pron: awldis) 'from the largest house'. Var. and dim., Aldas, Aldus, Aida.

ALDORA (Greek. Pron: aldora) 'winged gift'. Var. and dim., Aidorra, Alda, Dora.

ALERIS (Greek) 'from a city near the sea'. Var. and dim., Aleras, Alleras, Alleris, Allerus, Allerie, Ally.

ALETHEA (Greek. Pron: aleethia) 'truth'. Var. and dim., Aleethea, Alitha, Letha, Litha, Lithea, Aletheia, Alatea.

ALETTA (Latin) 'graceful as a bird'. Var. and dim., Aleta, Alitta, Alita, Letta, Litta.

ALEXANDRA (Greek) 'helper'. Feminine of Alexander. Var. and dim., Alexa, Alexandrina, Alexina, Alexine, Alexis, Alix, Alla, Elexa, Sandra, Sandi, Sandie, Sandy, Sandra.

ALEXIA (Greek) 'helper'.

ALDREDA (Old German) 'elf counsel'. Feminine of Alfred. Dim., Ally.

ALICE (Old French–German) 'noble and kind'. Var. and dim., Alicia, Alisa, Alison, Allissa, Aleece, Alyce, Allis, Alis, Elissa, Alla, Allie, Ally, Alys.

ALIENOR (Greek. Pron: alleeaynor) 'light'.

ALINA (Old German) 'noble'. Var. and dim., Alena, Alinna, Alius, Alli, Ally, Lina, Aline, Alyna, Lana.

ALISON (Old German) Diminutive of Alice used as a name in its own right. Var. and dim., Alisan, Allison, Ali, Alicen.

ALMA (Latin) 'loving and kind' or 'fair'.

ALMEDHA (Welsh. Pron: almeeda) 'shapely'.

ALMETA (Latin) 'very industrious'. Var. and dim., Almeeta, Almita, Almitta, Alma, Mita.

ALMIRA (Arabic) 'princess; the exalted'. Feminine of Elmer. Dim., Mira.

ALODIE (Old English) 'rich'. Var. and dim., Alodee, Alodi, Alo, Lodie, Lody.

ALOYSIA (Old German) 'famous war'. Var and dim., Aloisia, Alyose, Lois.

ALTHEA (Greek) 'wholesome; healing'. Var. and dim., Altheta, Althee, Thea.

ALVA (Latin) 'white; fair'.

ALVINA (Old German). Feminine of Alvin. Dim., Vina.

ALVITA (Latin) 'alive; vivacious'. Var. and dim., Alveta, Allveta, Veta, Vita.

ALWYN (Old German) 'elf friend'.

ALYSIA (Greek 'noble cheer'. Var., Alisa, Alisia, Alysa.

AMABEL (Latin) 'lovable'. Var. and dim., Amabelle, Amabil, Ama.

AMALA (Lombardic) 'work'.

AMALINA (Gothic) 'work' and 'serpent'.

AMANDA (Latin) 'fit to be loved'. A 17th-century literary invention. Var. and dim., Manda, Mandy.

AMARIS (Hebrew. Pron: amaris) 'God hath promised good'. Var. and dim., Amaras, Amari, Amary, Mari, Maris.

AMARYLLIS Greek. Pron: amahrilis) used by Greek poets as a name for country girls. Var. and dim., Amarilas, Amarillis, Ama, Amaryl, Maryl, Rillis.

AMATA (Latin. Pron: amahta) 'beloved'.

AMBER (Arabic) 'jewel'.

AMBROSINE (Greek). Var. and dim., Ambrosane, Ambrosia, Amber, Brosine, Brosy.

AMELIA (Old German) 'industrious, striving'. Feminine of Emil. Var. and dim., Amalia, Amelie, Mell, Mellie, Mill, Millie. See also **EMILY**.

AMETHYST (Greek) The name of the purple precious stone. Var., Amathist, Amathiste, Amethist.

AMICE (Latin. Pron: amees) very popular name in England from the 12th to the 15th century. The meaning is uncertain. Var., Amicia.

AMINTA (Greek) 'protected'.

AMITY (Latin) 'friendly'. Var. Amati, Amaty.

AMORETTE (Latin) 'beloved'. Var. and dim., Amarette, Amorete, Amora, Moretta, Morette.

AMORITA (Latin) 'beloved'. Var., Amoreta, Amoritta.

AMY (Old French) The past participle of the verb, to love. Var., Aimée, Ami, Amie, Amata, Ayme, Amia.

ANASTASIA (Greek) 'who will rise again'. Var. and dim., Ana, Stacey, Stacy, Tasia, Tasa.

ANATOLA (Greek. Pron: anatola) 'of the East'. Feminine of Anatole.

ANCELLA (Greek. Pron: ansela) 'angel'. Var. and dim., Ancalin, Ancilin, Ancel, Celin, Celine.

ANCHORETTE (Welsh. Pron: ankawret) 'much loved'. Var., Ancret, Ancreta, Anchet.

ANCILLA (Latin. Pron: ansila) 'handmaiden'. Var., Anzella, Ansela.

ANDREA (Italian. Pron: andreeya) 'womanly'. Femi-

13

nine of Andrew. Var. and dim., Andre, Andee, Andi, Andy.

ANDRINA Found often in Scotland along with the clumsier Andrewina.

ANDROMEDA (Greek) 'the justice of the Lord'. Var. and dim., Andromada, Andromede, Andra, Andromea, Andy, Meda.

ANGELA (Greek) 'messenger', 'angelic'. Var. and dim., Angeline, Angelita, Angel, Angie, Angy, Angeletta.

ANGELICA (Latin) 'angelic'.

ANGELINA dim. of Angela, used as a name in its own right.

ANISIA (Greek) 'complete'.

ANITA (Hebrew) 'grace'. A form (originally Spanish) of Ann. Var. and dim., Anita, Aneta, Nita.

ANN (Hebrew) 'whom God has favoured'. Western form of the Hebrew Hannah. Var. and dim., Anna, Anne, Annetta, Annette, Annie, Annora, Nan, Nana, Nancy, Nanete, Nanette, Nanine, Nanon, Nina, Ninette, Ninon.

ANNABEL probably Scottish variation of the Latin Amabel, 'lovable'.

ANNAROSE Irish mixing of Anna and Rose.

ANONA see NONA.

ANNOT (English. Pron: ano) dim. of Agnes sometimes used as a name in its own right.

ANSELA see ANCILLA.

ANSTICE (Old English. Pron: anstis) 'resurrection'.

ANTHEA (Greek) 'like a flower'. Var. and dim., Anthia, Bluma, Thea, Thia.

ANTIGONE (Greek, Pron: antigoni) 'contrary'; 'born against'.

ANTONIA (Latin) 'inestimable'. Feminine form of Anthony. Var. and dim., Antonia, Antoni, Antoinetta, Antoinette, Toinette, Toni, Netta, Nettie, Netty.

APHRA (Old German) 'A greeter of people'. Var., Afra.

APPLE The name of the fruit, sometimes used as a Christian name.

APRIL (Latin) The name of the month, used as a Christian name in recent times.

ARABELLA (Latin) 'from Arabia' or 'easily entreated'. Var. and dim., Arabelle, Ara, Bel, Bell, Bella, Belle.

ARAMINTA (Hebrew) 'elegant'. Var. and dim., Aramanta, Aramenta, Aramin, Ara.

ARETA (Greek) 'virtuous rule'. Var. and dim., Aretta, Arette, Aretina, Aret, Reta, Tinaret.

ARIADNE (Greek) 'the very holy one'. Var., Ariana, Ariane.

ARIANWEN (Welsh) 'silver'.

ARMINEL (Old English) A name found in Devon and Cornwall. Meaning uncertain.

ASBERA (Old German. Pron: azbera) 'divine bear'.

ASPASIA (Greek. Pron: aspayzia) 'welcome'.

ASTA (Latin) 'venerable'.

ASTRID (Norse) 'God's strength'.

ATALANTA (Greek) 'swift runner'. Var. and dim., Atalante, Atalanti, Attalanta, Talanta, Tala.

ATALAYA (Spanish–Arabic) 'watchtower'. Var. and dim., Ataliah, Atalya, Atalayah, Atal, Talya.

ATALIE (Scandinavian) 'pure'. Var., Atalee, Attalie, Talie.

ATHENE (Greek) 'wise; wisdom'. Var., Athene.

AUDREY (English. Pron: awdri) 'noble threatened'. Var. and dim., Audrie, Audry, Audie, Dee.

AUDRIS (Old German) 'fortunate'. Var., Audras, Audres, Audrit, Andrye.

AUGUSTA (Latin) 'majestic, venerable'. Feminine of August. Var. and dim., Augustina, Augustine, Austina, Austine, Gusta, Gussie, Tina.

AURELIA (Latin. Pron: Awreelia) 'golden'. Var. and dim., Aura, Aurea, Aurora, Aurelie, Aurel, Aurie, Ora, Orel, Oralia, Oralie.

AURIOL see **ORIOLE**.

AURORA (Pron: awrawra) The Latin name for the goddess of the dawn.

AVA see **AVIS**.

AVELINE (Norman. Pron: aveleen) 'pleasant'.

AVERIL (Old English) 'wild boar; battle maiden'.

AVICE (Latin. Pron: ayvis) 'a bird'. Var. and dim., Ava, Avi, Avis, Aricia.

AZALEA (Old German. Pron: azaylia) 'noble cheer'. Var. and dim., Azaleah, Azelea, Azal, Zela, Zalea.

AZARIA (Hebrew. Pron: azahria) 'blessed by God'. Var. and dim., Azariah, Azeria, Azerria, Azar, Zaria, Zerr.

B

BABETTE see **ELIZABETH**.

BAPTISTA (Greek) 'baptized in God's name'.

BARBARA (Greek) 'strange, foreign'. Var. and dim., Babby Babs, Barby.

BASILIE, BASILIA (Greek) 'majestic'.

BATHSHEBA (Hebrew. Pron: bathsheeba) 'voluptuous'. Var. and dim., Bathsheb, Bathsheeb, Sheba.

BEATA (Latin. Pron: Beeta) 'happy'. Dim., Bea.

BEATRICE (Latin. Pron: beeatris) 'bringer of joy'. Var. and dim., Beatrix, Bea, Bee, Bice, Trix, Trixie.

BECKY see **REBECCA**.

BEKA (Hebrew) 'half-sister'. Var., Becca, Bekka, Bekah.

BELDA (French) 'lovely woman'. Var. and dim., Bellda, Belldame, Belldas, Belle.

BELLA, BELLE see **ISABEL.**

BELINDA (Italian) 'wise serpent'. Dim., Bel, Linda, Lindie Lindy.

BELLONA (Old English. Pron: belona) 'warlike'.

BENA (Hebrew) 'wise'. Var., Beena, Benah, Bina.

BENEDICTA (Latin) 'blessed'. The Feminine of Benedict. Var., Benedetta, Benetta, Benita.

BENITA see **BENEDICTA.**

BENYNA (Latin. Pron: beneena) 'kind'.

BERNADETTE (Old German) 'brave; strong'. The feminine of Bernard. Made popular by St. Bernadette of Lourdes and sometimes used in the British Isles. Var. and dim., Bernadina, Bernadine, Berneta, Bernetta, Bernette, Berni, Bernie.

BERNADINE see **BERNADETTE.**

BERNICE (Macedonian) 'bringer of victory'. Var. and dim., Berenice, Berni, Berny.

BERTHA (Old German) 'shining bright'. Var. and dim., Berta, Bertina, Berti, Bertie.

BERTILLA (Latin) 'kind and shy'. Var. and dim., Bertila, Tilla, Tilly.

BERYL (Greek. Pron: beril) The name of a precious stone. Var. and dim., Beryle, Berri, Berrie, Berry.

BESS, BESSE, BESSIE see **ELIZABETH.**

BETHIA (Hebrew. Pron: beethia) 'worshipper of God'.

BETH (Gaelic) 'life'. See also **ELIZABETH.** Var., Bethia.

BETHESDA (Hebrew) 'from a place of fountains'. Var. and dim., Bethesde, Beth, Thessa.

BETSY, BETTE, BETTY see **ELIZABETH.**

BETTINA (Latin) 'blessed'.

BEULAH (Hebrew) 'she who will be married'. Var. and dim., Beula, Beulie.

BEVERLY (Old English) 'ambitious'. Var. and dim., Beverley, Beverlie, Bev, Bevvy.

BIANCA Italian form of Blanche.

BICE see **BEATRICE.**

BITHIA (Hebrew) 'given to God'. Var., Bitthia.

BLANCHE (French. Pron: blahnch) 'fair, white'. Var., Bianca, Blanca, Blanch, Branca.

BLODWEN (Welsh) 'white flower'.

BONNIE (Latin) 'sweet and good'. Var., Boni, Bonne, Bonni, Bonny.

BRENDA A Shetland name taken from the Norse 'firey'.

BRENNA (Celtic) 'black haired'.

16

BRIANNA (Celtic. Pron: brianna) 'woman of strength'. Var. and dim., Briana, Bria.

BRIDGET (Celtic. Pron: brijit) 'the high one', or 'strength'. Var. and dim., Bridgid, Brigette, Brigida, Brigitte, Brieta, Brietta, Brita, Brie.

BRIDIE (Scottish. Pron: bridi) 'strength'.

BRIETTA see **BRIDGET**.

BRITANNIA sometimes used as a woman's name in the 18th century.

BRONESSA The Welsh 'white' with an English suffix.

BRONWEN (Welsh) 'white breast'. A common name in Wales.

BRUCENA (Scottish. Pron: bruseena) Feminine of Bruce, the name of the liberator – king of Scotland.

BRYONY (Irish. Pron: brioni) 'strong'.

C

CAIETA (Latin. Pron: kieta) 'rejoiced in'.

CAITLIN (Welsh. Pron: kaytlin) 'done'.

CALELLA Maybe a contraction of Celtic, 'handmaid'.

CALISTA (Greek) 'most lovely'. Var. and dim., Callista, Calise, Allista, Alisa.

CAMILLA (Latin) 'attendant at a sacrifice'. Var. and dim., Camella, Camellia, Camille, Cam, Kamala, Milly.

CANDACE (The dynastic title of the queens of Ethiopia). Var. and dim., Candice, Candie, Candy.

CANDIDA (Latin) 'white'.

CARA (Celtic) 'friend'.

CARISSA (Latin) 'schemer'. Var. and dim., Carisa, Carl, Chrissa, Crissa.

CARITTA (Latin. Pron: kareeta) 'generous'. Var. and dim., Carita, Cari, Rita.

CARLA (Italian) 'woman'. A feminine form of Charles. Var. and dim., Karla, Carly, Karly.

CARLOTTA (Italian) 'one who is strong'. Another feminine form of Charles.

CARMELA (Hebrew) 'garden'. Var., Carmel, Carmelita.

CARMEN (Latin) 'vineyard'. Var. and dim., Carmena, Carmina, Carmine, Carmita.

CAROL (French) 'a woman'. A version of Charles. Var. and dim., Carole, Carolle, Caryl, Karol, Karole, Carey, Carrie, Cary.

CAROLINE (Old German–English) 'a woman'. The feminine of Charles. Var. and dim., Carola, Carolina, Carolyn, Karolina, Karoline, Karolyn, Carrie, Lina.

CAROMY (Pron: karomi) Maybe a diminutive of Celtic, 'friend'.

CASILDA (Spanish) 'the solitary one'. Var. and dim., Casilde, Cassilda, Cassi, Cassil, Silda.

CASSANDRA (Greek) 'the name of a prophet'. Var. and dim., Cassandre, Cass, Cassie, Cassy, Sandi, Sandy.

CATHERINE, CATHERINA, CATHARINE, CATHLEEN see KATHERINE.

CATRIONA The Gaelic diminutive of Katherine.

CECILIA (Latin) St. Cecilia martyred in A.D. 177 is the patron saint of music. Var. and dim., Cecile, Cecily, Celia, Cicely, Cicily, Cis, Cissy.

CELESTE (Latin) 'heavenly'. Var., Celesta, Celestine.

CELIA A form of Cecilia used by Shakespeare in *As You Like It* for the name of Rosalind's cousin.

CERELIA (Latin. Pron: sereelia) 'fruitful woman'. Var. and dim., Cerellia, Cerallua, Cerell, Cerelly, Erelia.

CERIDWEN (Welsh. Pron: seridwen) 'fair poetry'. Found often in Wales.

CHARIS (Greek) 'grace'. Var., Clarissa.

CHARITY (English) 'love'. Var. and dim., Charita, Charry, Cherry.

CHARLESEMA (Scottish. Pron: chahlseema) Scottish feminization of Charles.

CHARLOTTE (Italian) 'womanly'. Another feminine form of Charles. Var. and dim., Carlotta, Charlene, Charline, Carry, Letty, Lotta, Lotte, Lottie, Lotty.

CHARMAINE (Pron: shamayn). May have become popular after the song of that name.

CHARMIAN (Greek) 'a little joy'.

CHERITH (English) 'cherish'.

CHERYL (English) 'love'. Var., Cherry.

CHLOE (Greek) 'a young green shoot'.

CHLORIS (Greek) 'blooming, fresh'. Var. and dim,. Chloras, Chlores, Chiori, Lori, Loris.

CHRISTABEL (Latin. Pron: kristabel) 'beautiful in Christ'.

CHRISTIANA see CHRISTINE.

CHRISTINE (Old English) 'Christian'. The feminine of Christian. Var. and dim., Christa, Christiana, Christina, Christabelle, Christal, Chrystal, Crystal, Kristiana, Kristina, Kristine, Chris, Chrissie, Chrissy, Tenna, Tina.

CILLA (Latin. Pron: Sila) 'blind'.

CINDY see CYNTHIA.

CLAIRE, CLARE see CLARA.

CLARA (Latin) 'bright, shining'. Var., Claire, Clare, Clareta, Clarette, Clarine, Clarinda.

CLARABELLE (Latin–French) 'bright, shining, beautiful'. Var., Claribel.

CLARICE French variation of Clara. Var., Clarissa, Clarise.

CLARIMOND (Old English–Latin) 'bright protection'.

CLARINDA variation of Clare used by Spenser in *The Fairie Queen*.

CLAUDETTE see CLAUDIA.

CLAUDIA (Latin) 'the lame' (this meaning has been obscured by time and usage). The feminine of Claud. Var. and dim., Claude, Claudette, Claudina, Claudine, Claudie.

CLEDRA (Cornish) meaning uncertain.

CLEMENCE (Hebrew) 'mildness'. Var. and dim., Clementas, Clemtina, Clementine, Clemen, Clementi, Cleti, Clemency.

CLEO (Greek) 'famed'.

CLEODEL (Greek) 'from a famous place'. Var. and dim., Cleodal, Cleodell, Cleo, Clee.

CLEONE (Greek. Pron: klioni) 'light', 'clear'.

CLEOPATRA (Greek) 'from a famous father'. Var. and dim., Cleopatre, Cleo.

CLODAGH (Irish. Pron: kloda). The name of a river in Tipperary.

CLORINDA see CLARINDA.

CLOTILDA (Old German) 'loud battle'.

CLOVER (Old English) 'holy fame' a name now associated with the wild flower.

COLETTE French diminutive

of Nicol, 'victory of the people'.

COLINETTE (English–Latin) 'dove'.

COLLEEN (Irish) 'maiden'. Var. and dim., Coleen, Colene.

COLUMBINE (Latin) 'dove'. Var., Columbyne.

CONSTANCE (Latin) 'unchanging, constant'. Var. and dim., Constantia, Constantina, Constantine, Con, Conni, Connie.

CORA (Greek) 'maiden'. Var. and dim., Corena, Coretta, Corette, Corianna, Corinne, Corena, Corrie, Corry.

CORAL (Greek) 'coral'. Var., Corel.

CORALIE A romantic name invented by the French after the revolution.

CORDELIA (Celtic) 'jewel of the sea'. Var. and dim., Cordalia, Cordeelia, Delia.

CORINNA (Greek) 'maiden'.

CORNELIA (Latin) 'horn'. Feminine of Cornelius. Var. and dim., Cornela, Nelia, Nela, Nell, Nellie, Nelly.

CORONATA (English. Pron: koronahta) a modern invention from 'crown'.

CRESSIDA (Latin. Pron: kresida) 'faithless'.

CRYSTAL sometimes used as a woman's name as are other beautiful or precious stones. Chrystal is a Scottish diminutive of Christopher.

CYNTHIA (Greek) Dim., Cindy, Cyn, Cynth, Cynthie.

CYRILLA (Greek) 'lordly'. Feminine of Cyril.

CYPRA (Latin) 'from Cyprus'. Feminine of Cyprian.

D

DACIA (Latin. Pron: daysia) 'from the far land'. Var. and dim., Dachia, Dashi, Dachy.

DAFFODIL (Greek) 'the tall white flower'. Var. and dim., Dafodil, Daffie.

DAGMAR (Danish) 'joy of the land'. Dim., Dag.

DAGNA (Norwegian) 'fresh as day'. Var. and dim., Daggna, Dagnah, Dag.

DAISY (English) Victorian pet name for Margaret (margarite-daisy).

DALIA (Hebrew. Pron: dahlia) meaning uncertain. Var., Dahlia.

DAMACIS (Greek) The name of an Athenian woman converted by St. Paul. Var. and dim., Damalas, Damales, Damalus, Damal, Damali.

DAMARA (Greek. Pron: Damahra) 'taming'. Var. and dim., Damarra, Damaris, Mara.

DANETTE (Hebrew) 'the Lord judges me'. Var. and dim., Danete, Danny.

DANICA (Slavonic) 'morning star'. Var. and dim., Dannica, Donica, Anica.

DANIELA (Hebrew) 'the judgement of God'. Feminine of Daniel. Var. and dim., Daniala, Danialah, Danni, Niela.

DAPHNE (Greek) 'laurel tree'. Dim., Daph, Daphie.

DARA (Hebrew) 'heart of my wife'. Var., Darra.

DARCY (Celtic) 'dark'. Var., Darcie, Dercy.

DARICE (Persian) 'queenly'. Var. and dim., Dareece, Darees, Dari.

DAVINA (Scottish) 'beloved'. Feminine of David. Var., Daveta, Davida, Davita.

DAWN This name is a 20th-century invention

DAYMER (Cornish) meaning uncertain.

DEANNA see **DIANA.**

DEBORAH (Hebrew) 'the bee'. Var. and dim., Debora, Debra, Deb, Debbie, Debby

DECEMBER (English) sometimes used for children born in that month.

DECIMA (Latin. Pron: desima) 'the tenth'.

DEIDRE (Irish) A name found in Irish tales and legends. Its meaning is uncertain. Var. and dim., Dierdre, Dedrie, Dee, Deedee.

DELENA see **DELIA.**

DELIA (Greek. Pron: deelia) derived from Delos the birthplace of Artemis. Var., Delena.

DELICIA (English. Pron: delisia) 'delightful'.

DELILAH (Hebrew) 'the temptress'. Var. and dim., Dalila, Lila, Lilah.

DELLA (Old German) 'of nobility'. Dim., Del.

DELORA (Latin) 'from the seashore'. Var. and dim., Dellora, Ellora.

DELPHINE (Greek) 'calmness, serenity'.

DELYTH (Hebrew) maybe 'lily'.

DEMELZA name taken from a remote Cornish hamlet.

DENIA (Greek) 'of Dionysius'.

DENISE (French from Greek) St. Denis is the patron saint of France. The feminine of Dennis. Var., Denice, Denys.

DESDEMONA (Greek) 'sorrowful'. Var. and dim., Desdamona, Desdamonna, Desdemonna, Demona, Desdee, Desdie, Mona.

DESIREE (French–Latin) 'desired'. Var., Desirea, Desireah.

DEVONA (Old English) 'brave'. Var. and dim., Devonna, Devina, Devinna, Deva, Yona.

DIANA The Latin name for the Goddess of the moon. Var. and dim., Deanna, Diane, Dianna, Di.

DIANE see DIANA.

DIELLA (Latin) 'holy girl'. Var., Dielle.

DILYS (Welsh. Pron: dilis) 'perfect, genuine, certain'.

DINAH (Hebrew) 'law suit'. The name of the daughter of Jacob.

DIONE (Greek) 'the daughter of heaven and earth'. Dim., Dionetta.

DISA (Norwegian. Pron: deesa) 'active spirit'.

DITTA (French. Pron: dita) 'spoken'.

DOLORES (Latin) 'our Lady of Sorrows'. Var. and dim., Delores, Deloris, Dolora, Dori, Dorrie, Dorry.

DOMINICA (Latin. Pron: dominika) 'of the Lord', a name sometimes given to children born on Sunday. Var. and dim., Domineca, Domini, Dominik, Nica.

DONATA (Latin. Pron: donahta) 'gift'.

DONELLA (Latin) 'little girl'. Var. and dim., Donela, Donell, Nell.

DONNA (Italian) 'lady'.

DONNET (Latin. Pron: donet) 'given'. A name sometimes found in Cornwall.

DORA see DOROTHY.

DORCAS (Greek) 'gazelle'. Var. and dim., Dorcea, Dorcia, Dorca, Dorcy.

DOREEN maybe an Irish variation of Dorothy. Var. and dim., Dorine, Dori, Dorie, Dory.

DORINDA An 18th-century

21

invention modelled on Belinda and Clarinda supposedly taken from the Greek 'gift'.

DORIS The name of a sea nymph in Greek mythology. Dim., Dodi.

DOROTHEA, DOROTHY (Greek) 'gift of God'. A feminine form of Theodore. Var. and dim., Dora, Doretta, Dorothi, Dorthea, Dorthy, Dee, Dolley, Dollie, Dolly, Dore, Dot, Dottie, Dotty.

DRUSILLA (Latin) The feminine of Drusus. The name of a Roman patrician family.

DUKANA (Irish. Pron: dyu-kahna) 'Servant of Maedoc' (Marmaduke was sometimes shortened to Duke. Dukana is the feminine form.)

DULCIE (Latin) 'sweet'. Var., Dulci, Dulcine, Dulcinea.

DUMA (Hebrew. Pron: dyu-ma) 'quiet, a gentle woman'. Var. and dim., Dhumma, Dumah, Dhu.

DYMPNA (Irish) 'fit to be'. Var., Dymphna.

E

EASTER (Old English) sometimes used as a Christian name, like Christmas and Pascal.

ECHO (Greek) 'echo'.

EDA see EDITH.

EDANA see EDITH.

EDEN (Hebrew) 'enchanting'.

EDITH (Old German) 'rich war'. Var. and dim., Eadith, Eda, Edythe, Eadie, Ede, Edie.

EDMEE (Old English) 'the fortunate protector'. Var. and dim., Edme, Edmea, Emee, Eda, Edana.

EDNA (Hebrew) meaning uncertain. The name occurs in the books of *The Apocrypha*.

EDRA (Hebrew) 'woman of power'. Var. and dim., Edrea, Edris, Eddra, Ed.

EDWINA (Old English) 'valued friend'. Feminine of Edwin. Var. and dim., Eadwina, Eadwine, Edwine, Win, Wina, Winnie, Winny.

EFFIE see EUPHEMIA.

EGLANTYNE (Latin) 'prickly'. Another name for the sweetbriar. Var. and dim., Eglanteen, Eglantine, Glanti, Lanti, Aylente.

EIA (Celtic. Pron: ia) Early Christian saint who gave her name to the town of St. Earth in Cornwall.

EILEEN see AILEEN.

EITHNE (Old Irish. Pron: ethni) 'fire'.

ELAINE (Old English form of Helen). Var. and dim., Alaine, Alayne, Elana, Elayne, Laine, Lani.

ELDRIDA (Old English. Pron: eldreeda) 'the wise friend'. Var. and dim., Eldreda, Eldreeda, Dreda, Dreeda, Drida.

ELEANOR, ELEANORA, ELEANORE, ELENORE, ELINOR, ELNORE, ALIENOR. Provençal forms of Helen introduced into England by Eleanor of Aquitaine.

ELECTRA (Greek) 'brilliant star'. Dim., Lectra.

ELENA see **HELEN**.

ELFREDA (Old English. Pron: elfreeda) 'elf strength'. A feminine form of Albert. Var., Elfrida.

ELGIVA (Old English. Pron: elgeeva) 'elf gift'.

ELISE see **ELIZABETH**.

ELITA (Latin. Pron: eleeta) 'select, a special person'. Var. and dim., Ellita, Elie, Lita, Litta.

ELIZA see **ELIZABETH**.

ELIZABETH (Hebrew) 'God is my satisfaction'. Var. and dim., Elisa, Elisabeth, Elisabetta, Elise, Eliza, Elsa, Elsbeth, Elspeth, Else, Elsie, Lisabet, Lisabeth, Lisbeth, Ysabell, Isabell, Babette, Bess, Besse, Bessie, Bessy, Beth, Betsy, Bette, Betti, Bettina, Betty, Libby, Lisa, Lise, Liza, Lizzie, Lizzy, Tibby.

ELLA (Norman) 'all' (embracing). Var., Alia.

ELLEN The early English form of Helen. Var. and dim., Elen, Elene, Ellot, Elota, Ellota.

ELMINA (Old English. Pron: elmeena) 'myself'.

ELODIE (Greek) 'fragile flower'. Var. and dim., Elodea, Elodia, Ellie, Dee, Lodi, Lodie, Odie.

ELSA see **ELIZABETH**.

ELSA German diminutive of Elizabeth, sometimes used as a name in its own right.

ELSPETH, ELSIE see **ELIZABETH**.

ELVA (Old English) 'elfin'. Var., Elvia.

ELVINA (Old English) 'elf-friend'. Feminine of Elwin. Var., Elwina.

ELVIRA (Latin) 'white'. Dim., Elvie

ELVIVA (Old English) 'noble gift'. Var., Ailene.

EMERALD (English) The name of the precious green stone. Dim., Em, Emmy.

EMERENTIA (Latin) 'deserving'.

EMILY (Latin) from Aemilius, the name of a Roman family. A feminine form of Emil, Var. and dim., Emilia, Emillie, Em, Emmy, Millie.

EMMA (Old German) 'whole'. 'universal'. Dim., Em, Emie, Emmie, Emmy.

EMMELINE (Old French) probably 'industrious'.

EMILIETTA (Old German) diminutive of 'work serpent'.

ENA Anglicized version of the Irish Eithne, 'fire'.

ENID (Welsh) 'purity of soul'.

EPIFANIA (Greek) 'manifestation'.

ERDA (Old German) 'earth child'. Var., Erdah, Erdda

ERICA (Latin. Pron: erika) 'Heather'. Feminine of Eric. Var. and dim., Erika, Rica, Ricky, Rika, Riki.

ERINA (Irish) 'from Erin'. Var. and dim., Erin, Erine, Erinna, Erinne, Eri.

ERLINA (Old English). Var. and dim., Erleena, Erlinna, Erlinnas, Erlin, Lina.

ERMENGARDE (Old German) 'whole; universal' and 'strength'. Var., Ermyntrude, Armigil, Irmingard.

ERMINA (Latin) 'lordly', Var. and dim., Ermeena, Erminna, Erminia, Erma, Mina, Minna.

ERNESTINE (Old German) 'eagle stone'. Feminine of Ernest. Var. and dim., Erna, Ernesta, Teena, Tina.

ESMERALDA (Spanish) 'emerald'. Var. and dim., Esmerelda, Esmerolda, Esma.

ESME (Pron: esmay) 'loved'. Probably old French.

ESTELLE (French) 'a star'. Var. and dim., Estella, Stella, Stel, Stelle.

ESTHER (Hebrew) 'myrtle'. Var. and dim., Esta, Ester, Hester, Essie, Essy.

ETAIN (Irish) 'crown'.

ETHEL (Old German) 'noble'. Var., Ethyl.

ETELKA (Slavonic) 'noble'.

ETHELIA (Old English) 'noble strength'.

ETHELIND (Old German) 'noble serpent'. Var. and dim., Ethelinda, Ethylind, Ethel.

ETTA Diminutive of Henrietta, sometimes used as a name in its own right.

EUDORA (Latin) 'happy gift'.

EUFROSINA (Greek) 'mirth'.

EUGENIA (Greek) 'nobility', 'excellence'. Feminine of Eugene. Var. and dim., Eugenie, Gena, Gene, Genie, Gina.

EULALIA (Greek) 'sweet spoken'. Var. and dim., Eulaliah, Lalia.

EUNICE (Greek. Pron: yunis) 'good victory'. Var., Unis.

EUPHEMIA (Greek) 'worship of the Gods', 'honour' or 'good repute'. Var. and dim., Eupheemia, Euphemiah, Uphemia, Phemia.

EUSTACIA probably 'fruitful'. Feminine of Eustace. Dim., Stacy.

EVADNE (Hebrew) 'life'. Var. and dim., Evadnee, Eva, Vadnee.

EVANGELINE A name invented by Longfellow for his poem *Evangeline*, 'happy messenger'. Var., Evangelene, Evangelina, Evangelista.

EVANIA (Greek) 'child of peace'. Var. and dim., Evannia, Vania, Vani.

EVE (Hebrew) 'lively'. Var. and dim., Eva, Eveleen, Eveline, Evita, Evonne, Evie.

EVELINA, EVELYN (Old German) From the name Anita in Spain.

F

FABIA (Latin. Pron: faybia) 'bean grower'.

FAITH (Latin) Became common as a Christian name after the Reformation. Var., Fae, Fay, Faye.

FANNY (English) 'free'. Var., Fan, Fannie.

FARICA (Old German. Pron: fareeka) 'The peace-loving ruler'. Var. and dim., Farrica, Farika, Feriga, Arcia, Fari.

FAY, FAYE may be a diminutive of Faith, or the word jay, 'fairy'.

FEDORA (Greek, Pron: fedawra) 'a gift of heaven'. Var. and dim., Fedorra, Edora, Dora.

FELICIA (Latin. Pron: felisia) 'happy'. Feminine of Felix. Var., Felice, Felise.

FELICITY (Latin) 'happiness'.

FENELLA (Gaelic) 'white shouldered'. Var., Finola.

FERN (Greek) 'a feather', or 'delicate plant'. Var., Ferna, Fernas, Ferna.

FIDELIA (Latin) 'faithful woman'. Var. and dim., Fidelas, Fidelia, Fidellas, Fidellia, Fedela, Fidellis, Dela, Idel.

FILIPA (Greek) 'lover of horses'. Var. and dim., Filippa, Filli, Lippa.

FINNA (Norwegian. Pron: finα) 'white'.

FINOLA see **FENELLA**.

FIONA (Gaelic) 'fair', 'white'. Var. and dim., Phionna, Phiona, Fia, Phia, Phio.

FLAVIA (Latin) 'yellow-haired', 'blonde'.

FLEUR (French) 'flower'.

FLORA (Latin) The name of the Roman goddess of flowers.

FLORENCE (Latin) 'blooming'. Var. and dim., Fleur, Fleurette, Flora, Florette, Florinda, Floria, Floris, Flower, Flo, Flossie.

FLOWER This was occasionally used as a girl's name in the 17th century.

FORELLA either German 'fish' or an inversion of Flora.

FRANCES (Latin) 'a French woman'. Feminine of Francis. Var. and dim., France, Francesca, Francine, Fran, Franny.

FREDA see **WINIFRED**.

FREDELLA (Old German) 'peaceful elf'. Var. and dim., Fredela, Della.

FREDERICA (Old German) 'peaceful ruler'. Feminine of Frederick. Var., Fredrica. Fredrika.

FRODA (Norwegian) 'wise'.

FROMA (Old German) 'holy'. Var., Fromma, Fruma.

FRONIA (Latin. Pron: fronia)

'wise teacher'. Var. and dim., Fronnia, Fronniah, Onia.

FULVIA (Latin) 'yellow-haired'. Var. and dim., Fulviah, Fulvi, Via.

FYNVOLA (Scottish. Pron: finvola) 'fair shouldered'.

G

GABRIELLE (Hebrew) 'strong woman of God'. Feminine of Gabriel. Var. and dim., Gabriella, Gabey, Gabi, Gable.

GAENOR, GAYNOR see **GUINEVERE.**

GAIL, GALE see **ABIGAIL.**

GALATEA (Greek. Pron: galayshia) 'ivory'. Var. and dim., Galateah, Galetea, Galatia, Galitea, Alatea, Latea.

GALIENA (Old German) 'lofty'.

GARDA (Old German) 'enclosure'. Var. and dim., Gardas, Gardda, Gardia, Arda, Ardas, Ardis.

GARNET (English). The name of the semi-precious red stone.

GAVRA (Hebrew) 'the Lord is my rock'. Var. and dim., Gavrah, Garilla, Avra, Arilla.

GAY (origin uncertain) 'merry'. Var., Gae, Gaye.

GEMMA (Italian. Pron: Jemma) 'a gem'.

GENA, GENE, GINA see **EUGENIA, REGINA.**

GENEVIEVE (Celtic. Pron: jeneveev) 'white wave'.

GEORGIANA (Greek) 'tiller of the soil'. Feminine of George. Var. and dim., Georgetta, Georgette, Georgia, Georgianna, Georgina, Georgine, Georgi, Georgie.

GERALDINE (Old German) 'spear rule'. Feminine of Gerald. Var. and dim., Geraldina, Jeraldine, Geri, Gerri, Gerry, Jeri, Jerrie, Jerry.

GERMAINE (Pron: jermayn) French feminine of Germanus, a favourite saint of the Celto-Roman church. Dim., Gerrie.

GERTRUDE (Old German) 'spear strength'. Dim., Gerta, Gerti, Gerite, Gerty, Trude, Trudy.

GERVASE (Old German. Pron: jervayz) 'spear holder'. Sometimes used as a feminine name.

GETA (Latin. Pron: geeta) 'divine power'.

GILBERTA (Old German) 'bright pledge'. Feminine of Gilbert. Var. and dim., Gilbertine, Gilbertina, Gilpina, Wilberta, Gibera, Wilba, Wilbera.

GILDA (Celtic. Pron: jilda) 'God's servant'. Dim., Gilli.

GILLIAN (Latin) 'downy'. The popular feminine form of Julian. Var. and dim., Giliana, Giliane, Gilliet, Gilietta, Gilliette, Gillie.

GINEVRA (Pron: jinevra).

The Italian form of Guinevere occasionally used in the British Isles.

GISELA (Old German) 'a promise'. Var. and dim., Giselle, Gisele, Gissy, Giselda.

GITHA, GYTHA (Norse) probably from 'war'.

GLADYS Welsh form of the Latin Claudius, the name of a famous Roman family. Var. and dim., Gladine, Gladis, Glad, Gladdie.

GLENNA (origin uncertain) 'from the valley'. Feminine of Glenn. Var. and dim., Glenda, Glennis, Glynis, Glen, Glenn, Glennie.

GLORIA (Latin) 'glory'. Dim., Glory.

GLORIANA Gloria and Anna combined; thus, 'glorious grace'. Var., Glorianna.

GLYNIS see GLENNA.

GOODETH (Old English) 'God' and 'war'.

GRACE (Latin) 'grace'. Var. and dim., Gracia, Gracye, Gracie.

GRACILIA (Latin. Pron: Grasilia) 'slender'.

GRANIA (Irish) 'love'. Var. and dim., Graniah, Grannia, Granniah, Grannias, Grani.

GRATIANA (Latin. Pron: grashiahna) 'thankful'. Var. and dim., Gratianna, Gratiannah, Atlana, Grati, Tiana.

GREDEL, GRETA, GRETCHEN see MARGARET.

GREER (Greek) 'the watchwoman'.

GRETA A Swedish diminutive of Margaret. Sometimes used in the British Isles probably after the film star Greta Garbo.

GRISELDA (Old German) 'grey strife'. Dim., Grissel, Selda, Zelda.

GUINEVERE (Welsh. Pron: gwiniveea) 'fair lady'. Var. and dim., Guenevere, Jennifer, Gen, Genny, Jen, Jenni, Jennie, Jenny, Gaenor, Gaynor.

GURDA (Hebrew. Pron: geeda) 'praise'.

GWENDA (Welsh). A pet form of Gwendolen sometimes used as a Christian name in its own right.

GWENDOLEN (Welsh) 'white-browed' Var. and dim., Gwendolyn, Gwen, Gwenn, Gwyn, Gwyneth, Wendi, Wendy.

GWENEAL (Celtic) 'white angel'.

GWENYDD (Welsh) 'white'.

GYTHA (English. Pron: githa) 'gift'.

H

HAIDEE (Pron: Hayday). 'to caress'. Byron's version of Greek Haido.

HANNAH (Hebrew. Pron: hana) 'God has favoured me'. For var. and dim., see ANN.

HARRIET (Old German) 'ruler of the home'. A feminine of Henry. Var. and dim., Harrietta, Harriette, Hatti, Hattie, Hatty.

HAZEL (English). The name of the nut-bearing tree.

HEATHER (English). The name of the purple flowering plant.

HEBE (Greek. Pron: heebi) 'goddess of Spring'. Var., Hebbe.

HEDDA (Old German) 'war'. Var., Hedy, Heddy.

HELEN (Greek) 'light'. Var. and dim., Helena, Helene, Hellene, Eleanor, Eleanora, Eleanore, Elena, Elene, Elenore, Elinor, Elinore, Alienor, Ella, Ellen, Elnore, Lenore, Leonora, Leonore, Leora, Lora, Lorine, Ellie, Lenni, Lennie, Nell, Nellie, Nelly, Nora, Nella.

HELGA (Norse) 'holy'.

HELOISE see **LOUISE**.

HELSA (Hebrew) 'given to God'. Var. and dim., Hellsa, Hellsah, Helse, Hels, Els, Elsa, Helsie.

HENDRA (Cornish) 'ancient'.

HENRIETTA (Old German) 'home ruler'. A feminine form of Henry. Var. and dim., Henriette, Henrika, Enrica, Etta, Etty, Hennie, Hetti, Hetty.

HEPHZIBAH (Hebrew. Pron: hepzibah) 'my joy is in her'. Var. and dim., Hephzipa, Hepsiba, Hepsibah, Hepza, Hepzi, Zipah.

HERA (Greek) 'queen of the Gods'. Var., Herra, Herrah.

HERMIA (Greek. Pron: hermia). The feminine form of Hermes, the messenger of the gods.

HERMOINE (Greek. Pron: hermioni). A derivative of Hermes used by Shakespeare in *A Winter's Tale*. Var. and dim., Hermanda, Hermandine, Hermia, Irma.

HERO (Greek) 'earth mother'. Maybe from the name of the goddess Hera.

HERTHA (Old German Pron: Herta) 'earth mother'. Var., Eartha.

HESTER (Greek). The name of the goddess of the hearth.

HILARY (Latin) 'cheerful'. Var. and dim., Hillaria, Hillari, Hillary, Hilar.

HILDA (Old English) 'battle-maiden'. Var. and dim., Heidi, Hildie, Hildy.

HILDEBRAND (Old German) 'battle sword'

HILDEGARD (Old German) 'protecting battle-maiden'. Var. and dim., Hildagard, Hildegarde, Hilda, plus all dim., of Hilda.

HIPPOLYTA (Greek). The name of the queen of the Amazons.

HOLLY (Old English) 'good luck'. Var., Hollie.

HONORA (Latin. Pron: ona-wra) 'reputation' 'beauty'. Var. and dim., Honey, Hanoriz, Nora, Norah. Noreen, Norine, Norrie, Honora, Onara, Ion-nora.

HOPE (English) 'hope'.

HORATIA (Latin). The name of a famous Roman family.

HORTENSE (Latin). Name taken from a Roman family. Var., Hortensa, Hortensia, Or-tensa.

HULDA (Norse) 'muffled'.

HYACINTHE (Greek) 'purple'.

I

IANTHE (Greek. Pron: ian-thi) 'violet flower'. Dim., Ian.

IDA (Old Norse) 'labour'. Var., Idalla, Idelle.

IDONA (Old Norse). The name of the goddess of spring. Var. and dim., Idonah, Idonna, Donna, Idonea.

IDYLLA (Greek. Pron: Idila) 'perfection'.

IGNACIA (Latin. Pron: ignaycia) 'ardent'. Feminine of Ignatius. Var., Ignatia, Ignat-zia.

ILARIA (Latin) 'cheerful'.

ILITTA (Greek. Pron: ileeta) maybe diminutive of 'downy'.

ILONA (Greek. Pron: ilona) 'light'.

IMELDA (Latin) 'wistful'. Var. and dim., Imalda, Im-mellda, Imulda, Malda, Melda, Mella, Melly.

IMOGEN (Old Irish. Pron: imogen) 'daughter; girl'.

INA see **KATHERINE**.

INARET (Welsh) 'much loved'.

INEZ (Greek) 'peace'. Var., Ines.

INGRID (Old Norse) from the hero-name 'Ingri', and 'to ride'. Var., Inga, Ingeborg.

IOLA (Greek) 'downy'.

IONA (Scottish) The name of one of the Western Isles.

IRENE (Greek) 'peace'.

IRIS (Greek) 'rainbow'.

IRMA (Old German) 'strong'. Var. and dim., Erma, Erme, Irmina, Irmine, Irme.

IRMINGARD see **ERMEN-GARDE**.

ISA (Scottish). Pet form of Isabel.

ISABEL (French and Spanish version of Elizabeth). Originally from the name Elizabeth. Var. and dim., Isabella, Isa-belle, Isbel, Isobel, Bel, Bella, Belle.

ISADORA (Greek. Pron: eesa-dawra) 'strong gift'. Feminine of Isidore. Var. and dim., Isi-dora, Dora, Dori, Dory, Issy, Izzy.

ISLA (Scottish) May mean literally 'from the Isles'.

ISLEAN (Celtic. Pron: ileen)

'sweetvoiced'. Var. and dim., Islaen, Isleen, Isla.

ISMAY (Pron: ismay). A rare name used in the 13th century. Var., Ysmay, Isamaya.

ISMENIA maybe of Celtic origin. The meaning is uncertain (it is not connected to the Greek Ismene).

ISOLDA (Old German) 'ice rule'. Var., Isolde.

ISOLINE (Celtic) 'fair'.

IVANNA (Hebrew. Pron: ivana) 'God's gracious gift'. Feminine of Ivan, Var. and dim., Ivana, Ivanah, Iva, Ivie.

IVY A 19th-century innovation when flower and plant names became fashionable.

J

JAALA (Hebrew) 'wild she goat'. Var. and dim., Jaalla, Jala, Jaela, Jaella, Jaal, Jael.

JACINDA (Greek) 'beautiful; comely'. Var., Jacenta.

JACINTH (Greek) 'hyacinth'. It is also the name of a precious stone.

JACOBINA (Scottish) 'supplanter'. Feminine of Hebrew Jacob. Var. and dim., Jacobah, Jacoba, Jakoba, Jaco.

JACQUELINE (Hebrew) 'the supplanter'. Feminine of Jacques. Var. and dim., Jacquelina, Jaqueline, Jaquenetta, Jaquennete, Jackie, Jaquetta, Jaqui, Jakolina.

JADA (Hebrew) 'wise'. Var. and dim., Jadda, Jaddah, Ada, Addah.

JAEL see **JAALA**.

JAIRIA (Hebrew) 'enlightened by God'. Var. and dim., Jariah, Jari.

JAMESINA Scottish feminine form of James.

JAMILLA (Slavonic) 'Grace of the Lord'.

JANE (Hebrew) 'God has favoured'. Feminine of John. Var. and dim., Gianna, Janet, Janetta, Janette, Janice, Janis, Jayne, Jean, Jeanne, Jeanette, Jeannine, Joan, Joana, Joanna, Johanna, Juanita, Gian, Jan, Janey, Janie, Janna, Jeanie, Joanie, Jone, Jonie, Juana, Janeis.

JANET, JANETTE, JANICE see **JANE**.

JANETA Mediaeval diminutive of Jane.

JARITA (Hindu. Pron: jareeta) 'motherly bird'. Var. and dim., Gerita, Jeritah, Arita, Geri, Jari, Jeri, Rita.

JASIONE (Hebrew. Pron: jasioni). Feminine of Jason.

JASMIN (Persian) 'fragrant flower'. Var. and dim., Jasmine, Jasmina, Yasmin.

JEAN The modern Scottish form of Jane or Joan, from the Old French Jehane. Var. and dim., Jeanne, Jennet.

JEHANNE (Hebrew. Pron: jeyan) 'grace of the Lord'.

JEMIMA (Hebrew. Pron: jemima) 'dove'. Var. and dim., Jemena, Jeminah, Jemina, Jeminine, Jem, Jemmie, Mina, Minna.

JENEFER The Cornish spelling of Jennifer, see GUINEVERE.

JENNIFER see GUINEVERE.

JENNY Pet name for Jane; pronounced Jinny.

JERRI, JERRIE, JERRY see GERALDINE.

JESSAMINE (Hebrew) 'God is'.

JESSICA (Hebrew) 'He beholds'. Feminine of Jesse. Dim., Jess, Jesse, Jessi, Jessie, Jessy.

JESSIE A Scottish diminutive of Janet sometimes used as a name in its own right.

JEWEL (Latin) 'a precious stone'.

JILL pet form of Gillian often used as a name in its own right.

JOACHIMA (Hebrew) 'may God exalt'. Var. and dim., Joacima, Joacimah, Joshi.

JOAN see JANE.

JOANNA (Hebrew) 'the Lord's grace'.

JOCELYN (Old German) taken from the folk name 'Goth'. Var. and dim., Jocelin, Joslyn, Lyn, Lynn.

JODIE see JUDITH.

JOHANNA see JANE.

JOLETTA (English) from the Latin Viola, 'violette'.

JOSEPHINE (French–Hebrew) 'may God add' (children). Feminine of Joseph. Var. and dim., Josefa, Josepha, Josephina, Fia, Fifi, Jo, Josie.

JOY (Latin) 'joy'.

JOYCE (Celtic) The name of a 7th-century Breton saint.

JUDITH (Hebrew) 'Jewish woman'. Var. and dim., Juditha, Jodie, Jody, Judy.

JULIA (Greek) 'downy'. Feminine of Julius. Var. and dim., Juliana, Juliane, Juliet, Julietta, Juliette, Julie, Jill. Gillian.

JUNE (Latin) The name of the month, sometimes used as a Christian name in recent times.

JUNO (Latin. Pron: joono) 'queen of heaven'. Var. and dim., Jeno, Juna, Junna, Junno, Juni, Una, Uni, Uno.

JUSTINA (Latin) 'the just'. Feminine of Justin. Var. and dim., Justine, Tina.

JUTTA (Latin) 'spiritual'. Var. and dim., Jueta, Juetah, Juetta, Juta, Eta, Etta, Uta.

K

KAMALA see CAMILLA.

KAREN, KARIN, KARYN Danish form of Katherine.

KARLA see CARLA.

KAROL see CAROL.

KAROLINE, KAROLINA, KAROLYN see **CAROLINE.**

KASIA (Polish) 'pure'.

KATE see **KATHERINE.**

KATHERINE (Greek) maybe 'pure' or 'tortured'. Var. and dim., Catherina, Catherine, Cathleen, Karena, Katharina, Katherine, Katherin, Kathleen, Kathlene, Kathryn, Katrina, Catriona, Cassie, Ina, Kara, Kate, Kathie, Kathy, Katie, Kit, Kittie, Kitty, Kay.

KATHLEEN, KATHLENE see **KATHERINE.**

KATRINE Mediaeval spelling of Katherine.

KAY (Greek) 'rejoice' probably a Welsh form of the Latin Caius.

KELDA (Scandinavian) 'of a fresh mountain'. Var. and dim., Keldah, Kellda, Edla, Kela, Kella.

KENDRA (Old English) 'wise'. Var. and dim., Kendrah, Ken, Kendy.

KENTIGGERNA (Welsh) 'head chief'. Var. and dim., Kentigerma, Kentigera, Kentiga, Kenta, Kenti.

KETURAH (Hebrew. Pron: ketyurah) 'fragrance'.

KEZIA (Hebrew. Pron: kezia) The name of one of the daughters of Job. Found often in Cornwall.

KIKI A modern name, origin uncertain.

KIM (origin uncertain) 'noble or glorious leader'.

KIRSTEN (Scandinavian) 'the anointed one'.

KIRSTY Scottish diminutive of Christiana

KIT, KITTY see **KATHERINE.**

KOREN (Greek) 'young girl', Var., Koran, Korine.

L

LAELIA (Hebrew) 'devoted to the Lord'. Var. and dim., Lail, Lal, Lally.

LAIS (Greek) 'the adored'. Var., Laise, Laius.

LAETITIA see **LETTICE.**

LALAGE (Greek) 'babble'. Var. and dim., Lallage, Alage, Lala.

LALITA (Greek) 'frank'. Var. and dim., Lalitta, Lalittah, Lal, Lali, Lita.

LAMORNA (Cornish) 'leap jump'.

LANIVET (Cornish) 'religious place'.

LAODAMIA (Greek. Pron: layodahmia) 'people's tamer'.

LARA (Latin) 'famous'. Var., Larah.

LARENTIA (Latin) 'foster mother'. Var. and dim., Laurentia, Laurena.

LARINA (Latin) 'sea gull; girl of the sea'. Var. and dim., Lareena, Larena, Larine, Larrina, Lari, Rina.

LARISSA (Latin) 'happy'. Var. and dim., Laresa, Larisa, Larrisa, Arrisa, Lari, Laris, Risa, Rissa.

LATONIA (Latin) 'mother of the sun'. Var. and dim., Latona, Latoniah, Lattonia, Latia, Tonia.

LAURA (Latin) 'bay tree'. Feminine of Lawrence. Var. and dim., Laureen, Laurel, Lauren, Laurena, Laurinda, Laurencia, Lora, Loralie, Lorelie, Lorelle, Loren, Lorena, Loretta, Lorette, Lorinda, Lorine, Lorna, Lorne, Lari, Loree, Lori, Lore, Lorrie.

LAURENCIA see **LAURA**.

LAVERNE (French) 'spring-like'. Var. and dim., Laverna, Laverne, Verna, Verne, Vern.

LAVINA (Latin) meaning uncertain. The name of the second wife of Aeneas. Var. and dim., Lavina, Vina, Vinia.

LEAH (Hebrew) 'weary'. Var. and dim., Lea, Leigh.

LEANNE (English) combination of Lee and Ann. Var., Liana, Lianne.

LEATRICE (Latin) 'young and joyful'. Var. and dim., Liatrice, Liatris, Atrice, Leatri, Triss.

LEE (Old English) 'meadow'. Var., Lea.

LEILA (Persian) 'Moorish'. Var. and dim., Leilah, Leela, Lee.

LELA, LELAH, LELIA see **LILLIAN**.

LEMMUELA (Hebrew) 'dedicated to God'. Var. and dim., Lemuela, Lemuelah, Lemuella, Emmuela, Lem, Lemmie, Lemuel, Uela.

LENA, LINA (Greek) 'light'.

LENDA (Old German) may be a derivative of 'serpent'.

LEONA (Latin) 'the lion'. Feminine of Leo. Var. and dim., Leola, Leone, Leoni, Leonie, Lee, Lennie, Lenny.

LEONARDA (Old German) 'lion strong'. Feminine of Leonard.

LEONARA, LEONORE, LENORE see **HELEN**. May-be a form of Eleanor, came into use after Beethoven's opera *Fidelio*.

LEONTIA (Latin) 'lion-like'. Another feminine of Leo. Var. and dim., Leonteen, Leontina, Lyontine, Lee, Leo, Ontina, Ontine.

LEOPOLDINE (Germanic) 'of a bold people'. Feminine of Leopold. Var. and dim., Leopoldeeh, Denie, Dennie, Dian, Dine, Lea.

LESLEY (Celtic) A well known Scottish surname sometimes used as a Christian name. Feminine of Leslie. Var. and dim., Leslie, Lesli, Lesly, Les.

LETTICE, LAETITIA (Latin) 'gladness'. Var. and dim., Leticia, Leta, Lettie, Letty, Tish.

LETTIE, LETTY see **CHARLOTTE, LAETITIA**.

LEWINA (Hebrew) 'little prize of battle'. Var. and dim., Lawina, Leweena, Lewinia, Lewinna, Louina, Lew, Lewi, Lewin, Wina.

LIBBY see ELIZABETH.

LIDA (Slavonic) 'loved by all'. Var. and dim., Lidah, Lidda, Liddie.

LILA, LILAH, LILLA, see DELILAH, LILLIAN.

LILIA Scottish form of Lillian.

LILLIAN (Latin) Probably originated as a pet form of Elizabeth. Var. and dim., Lela, Lelah, Lelia, Lila, Lilah, Lilia, Lillian, Lillyan, Lil, Lilla, Lilli, Lillie, Lilly, Lily.

LILLITH (Assyro-Babylonian) 'goddess of storms'. Var. and dim., Lelith, Lilith, Lilithe, Lilli, Lillis.

LINA see CAROLINE.

LINDA (Old German) 'serpent'. Var. and dim., Lynda, Lind, Lindie, Lindy, Lynd.

LINETTE The mediaeval French form of the Welsh name Eluned, meaning uncertain. Var. and dim., Linetta, Linette, Lynette, Linn, Lynn, Netta, Nette.

LISA, LISE, LIZA, LIZZIE, LIZZY see ELIZABETH.

LISETTE, LISE, LIZZY, LISABET, LISABETH, LISBETH see ELIZABETH.

LIVIA see OLIVIA.

LLEWELLA see LUELLA.

LOIS (Old German. Pron: lois) 'famous war'. A feminine form of Louis.

LOLA Spanish diminutive of Dolores and Carlotta, sometimes used as a name in its own right. A feminine form of Charles. Var., Loleta, Lolita.

LOLITA see LOLA.

LORNA A name invented by the novelist R. D. Blackmore for the heroine of *Lorna Doone*.

LORELEI (Old German) The name of the water nymphs who lured travellers to their death in the River Rhine.

LORALIE see LAURA.

LORENA see LAURA.

LORETTA see LAURA.

LORINE see LAURA.

LORNA see LAURA.

LORRAINE (Old German) 'famous in battle'. Var., Laraine, Loraine.

LOTTA, LOTTIE, LOTTY see CHARLOTTE.

LOTUS (Egyptian. Pron: lotus) 'flower of forgetfulness'.

LOUISE (French) 'to hear' and 'to fight'. A feminine form of Louis. Var. and dim., Eloise, Heloise, Louisa, Lou.

LOVEDAY (English) Mediaeval name given to girls on a love day, or day of truce. It is still found in Cornwall.

LUCASTA A name invented by the poet Lovelace for the purpose of addressing his mistress who was a member of the Lucas family.

LUCILLE see **LUCY**. Var., Lucila.

LUCINDA A 17th-century poetic variation of Lucy.

LUCRETIA (Latin. Pron: lookreeshia). Feminine form of Lucretius, the name of a Roman family. Var., Lucree.

LUCY (Latin) 'light'. Feminine of Lucius. Var. and dim., Lucia, Lucilla, Lucille, Lucinda, Lucretia, Lucrece, Lucie, Lu.

LUDMILLA (Slavic) 'loved by all'. Var. and dim., Lodmilla, Lovmilla, Mila.

LUELLA (Latin) 'the appeaser'. Var., Lovella, Llewella.

LUNA (Latin) 'of the moonlight'. Var., Lunna.

LYANTI (Hebrew) meaning uncertain.

LYDIA (Greek) 'woman of Lydia'. Var. and dim., Lidia, Lydea, Lyda, Liddy.

LYNN a dim. of Evelyn, Madeline, etc., but used also as an independent name. Var., Lyn, Lynna, Lynne

LYNNET Maybe an English diminutive of Dutch, Lyntje, 'light'; or the name of the song bird.

M

MABEL (Latin) 'amiable, lovable'. Var. and dim., Mabelle, Maybelle, Belle, Mae.

MABYN (Welsh–Cornish. Pron: mabin) The name of three 6th-century saints. Var., Mahenna.

MADELINE (Hebrew) 'woman of Magdala'. Var. and dim., Madeleine, Madelene, Madelon, Magdalen, Magdalena, Magdalene, Magdaline, Marleen, Marlene, Marline, Maddie, Magda.

MADGE see **MARGARET**.

MADRA (Latin) 'mother'.

MAE see **MAY**.

MAFALDA (Latin) 'Princess of the poor'. Var. and dim., Mafolda, Mafela, Falda, Folda, Maffa.

MAGDA German abbreviation of Magdalena, sometimes used in the British Isles. See **MADELINE**.

MAGGIE see **MARGARET**.

MAGNA (Latin) 'great'. Var., Magnia.

MAGNOLIA (English) The name of the flowering tree, which may have been called after Mary of Magdala.

MAIDA (Old English. Pron: mayda) 'maiden'. Dim., Maidy.

MAIRE Irish form of Mary.

MAISIE Scottish diminutive of Margaret, now used as a name in its own right.

MALCA (Old German) 'active, industrious'. Var., Malcah.

MALISE (Gaelic. Pron: maleez) 'servant of Jesus'.

MALVA (Gaelic) 'handmaid'. Var. and dim., Malvia, Malviah, Malvie, Malvina.

MALVINA (Gaelic) 'smooth brow'. Var. and dim., Maleena, Mallina, Molina, Lina, Mali, Malin.

MANDA (Latin) 'of Magdala'.

MANNUELA (Hebrew. Pron: manyuela) 'God is with us'. Feminine of Emmanuel. Var. and dim., Emanuela, Emanella, Manella, Manuela, Ela, Uella.

MANON French diminutive of Marie. See **MARY**.

MARAH (Hebrew) 'bitter'.

MARCIA (Latin) 'of Mars'. Feminine of Mark. Var. and dim., Marcella, Marsha, Marcie, Marcy, Marcina.

MARCINA see **MARCIA**.

MARELDA (Old German) 'famous maid of war'. Var. and dim., Marolda, Mareld.

MARELLA (Old German) 'little'. Var. and dim., Marela, Marelya, Maria.

MARGARET (Greek) 'A pearl'. Var. and dim., Madge, Margarete, Margareta, Margery, Margo, Margot, Marjorie, Gredel, Greta, Gretl, Gretchen, Mag, Maggie, Maisie, Maizie, Marge, Margie, Meg, Peg, Peggy.

MARGERY, MARJORIE see **MARGARET** (a popular French form of Marguerite).

MARGO see **MARGARET**.

MARGUERITE see **MARGARET**.

MARIABELLA (Mediaeval) The Latin form of Mary, with 'beautiful' added.

MARIAMNE (Hebrew) a version of Miriam, sometimes used as a Christian name.

MARIANNE see **MARION**.

MARIE French form of Mary, sometimes used in the British Isles.

MARIEL Bavarian diminutive of Mary sometimes used in the British Isles. Var., Mariella.

MARIETTA, MARIETTE, MINETTE American names from the town Marietta in Ohio named after Queen Marie Antoinette.

MARIGOLDE (English) a modern name taken from the flower. It has not become popular.

MARILYN see **MARY**.

MARINA probably Latin 'of the sea'.

MARION was originally a diminutive of Mary. It was common in the Middle Ages. Var., Marian, Marianne.

MARIS (Latin) 'sea star'. Var. and dim., Marissa, Maras, Marris, Marus, Mari.

MARLA see **MARY**.

MARLEEN, MARLENE, MARLINE see **MADELINE**.

MAROLA (Latin. Pron: Marola) 'of the sea'. Var. and dim., Marala, Mareola, Arola, Maro, Ola.

MARSHA see **MARCIA**.

MARTHA (Aramaic) 'a chief'. Dim., Matty, Patty.

MARTINA (Latin) 'of Mars'. Feminine form of Martha.

MARY (Hebrew) 'long wished for child'. Var. and dim., Manon, Mara, Mari, Maria, Mariam, Marian, Marianne, Marie, Marietta, Mariette, Marilyn, Marion, Marla, Marya, Maureen, Minette, Miriam, Moira, Mairi, Mame, Mamie, Mimi, Minny, Mitzi, Mitzie, Moll, Mollie, Molly, Polly.

MATHILDA (Old German) 'strength in battle'. Var. and dim., Maud, Maude, Matti, Matty, Tilda, Tillie, Tilly.

MATTHIA (Hebrew) 'gift of God'. Var. and dim., Mathia, Mathiam, Methiam, Atthia, Mathi.

MAUDE (English) 'mighty battle maid'.

MAUNA (Latin. Pron: mawna) 'great'.

MAUREEN From the Irish Mairin, a diminutive of Mary.

MAURILIA (Latin) 'woman who sympathizes'. Var. and dim., Mauralia, Maurilias, Maurili, Maurie.

MAURITA (Latin) 'girl of the dark'. Var. and dim., Mauretta, Morita, Mourita, Aurita, Mauri, Rita, Urita.

MAVE (Irish) 'mirth'.

MAVIS Old English word for the song thrush. Var., Mavas.

MAWDWEN (Celtic) 'mannerly'.

MAXINE (Latin) 'greatest'. Feminine of Maximillian.

MAY modern pet form of Margaret or Mary, sometimes used as a name in its own right.

MAYDA (Old English) 'a maiden'. Var., Maida.

MAIZIE see **MARGARET**.

MEARA (Irish) 'merry'.

MEAVE The name of a legendary Irish Queen.

MEDARDA (Latin) 'student, scholar'. Var. and dim., Medardas, Darda, Dardas, Meda, Medar.

MEDORA (Old English) 'patient wife'. Var. and dim., Madora, Medorra, Dora, Edora, Medora, Ora.

MEDWENNA (Welsh) perhaps 'fair mannered'.

MEG see **MARGARET**.

MEGAN (Celtic) 'the strong'. Var., Meghan.

MELANELL (English) 'honey'.

MELANIE 'black'. Var. and dim., Melania, Malan, Melan, Mel, Mellie, Melly.

MELANTHA (Greek) 'dark flower'. Var. and dim., Melentha, Mela, Lantha.

MELESINA, MILICENT see **MILLICENT**.

MELINDA (Old German) 'work snake'.

MELIORA (Cornish) may mean 'better'. Var., Melior.

MELISSA (Greek) 'bee'. Var. and dim., Melisa, Lisa, Mel.

MELITA (Greek. Pron: mel-eeta) 'honey flower'. Var. and dim., Malita, Melleta, Melitta, Elita, Mali, Meli, Lita.

MELLONY see MELANIE.

MELODY (Somerset and Shropshire) 'melody'.

MELVINA (Celtic) 'chief'. Feminine of Melvin. Var. and dim., Malvina, Melba, Melina.

MERARI (Hebrew) 'girl of sadness, bitter'. Var. and dim., Meraree, Mera.

MERAS (Hebrew) 'worthy'. Var., Meris, Merras, Merus.

MERAUD (Cornish) possibly 'of the sea'.

MERCEDES (Spanish) 'Mary of Mercies'. Var. and dim., Mercedas, Merci, Mercy.

MERCY (English) came into use in the 17th century with other virtue names like Faith, Hope, and Charity.

MERLE (Latin) 'the blackbird'. Var. Meriel, Meri, Meria, Meryl.

MERUCIA (Pron: meroosia) An English inversion of Old Germany Merica 'work rule'.

MERIEL see MURIEL.

MERRIE (Old English) 'joyous, merry'. Var., Meri.

MERRIT (Old English) 'of merit'. Dim., Merri.

META (Latin) 'ambitious'. Var. and dim., Metta, Mettah, Mettas, Eta. Often found in Cornwall.

MIA (Latin) 'mine'.

MICHAELA (Hebrew. Pron: mikayala) 'in the image of God'. Feminine of Michael. Var. and dim., Michaele, Michaelina, Michella, Michellia, Mikaela, Mickie, Mickey, Mike, Miki.

MILDRED (Old English) 'mild strength'. Dim., Mil, Milli, Millie, Milly.

MILLICENT (Old German) 'work strong'. Var. and dim., Milicent, Melesina, Millicent, Milli, Millie, Milly.

MILLIE, MILLY see CAMILLA, EMILY, MILDRED, MILLICENT.

MIMI see MARY.

MINA pet name for Wilhemina.

MINELLA (Old English) 'helmet of resolution'.

MINERVA (Greek–Etruscan) The name of the Roman goddess of wisdom. Dim., Min, Minnie, Minny.

MINNA (Old German) 'loving memory' or 'little'. Dim., Min, Mini, Minnie, Minny.

MINNIE Scottish pet name for Mary now used as a name in its own right.

MIRABEL (Latin 'wonderful', 'glorious'. Var. and dim., Mirabelle, Mira, Bell, Belle.

MIRANDA (Latin) 'worthy of admiration'. Var. and dim., Miranda, Randa.

MIREILLE (Slavonic) 'bitter'.

MIRIAM see MARY.

MISELTA (Hebrew) possibly, 'who is like God'.

MOINA (Irish. Pron: moyna) possibly 'noble'. Var. and dim., Moyna, Moia, Moin, Oina.

MOIRA (Celtic) from the Irish form of Mary. Var. and dim., Maire, Moyra, Moir, Moya, Oira.

MOLLIE, MOLLY see **MARY.**

MONA (Irish) 'noble'.

MONDAY used as a Christian name in the Middle Ages for children born on the first day of the week.

MONICA possibly African, meaning uncertain. St. Monica was the mother of St. Augustine who was born in Carthage. Var., Monique.

MORAG (Gaelic) 'the sun'.

MORIA (Hebrew) 'chosen by the Lord'. Var. and dim., Moriah, Muriah, Mori.

MORGANA (Celtic. Pron: mawgahna) 'sea dweller'.

MORNA (Gaelic) 'beloved'. Var., Myrna.

MORVAH (Cornish) 'salt marsh'.

MORWENNA (Celtic) 'a wave of the sea'.

MURIEL (Celtic) 'sea bright'. Var. and dim., Meriel, Murielle, Mur.

MYRA (Latin) 'pearl'. Var., Mira.

MYRNA see **MORNA.**

MYRTLE The name of the shrub first used as a Christian name in the 19th century. Var. and dim., Myrtilla, Merta, Myrta, Mert, Myrt.

MYVANWY (Welsh) 'rare one' or 'child of the water'.

N

NADINE (French–Russian) 'hope'. Var. and dim., Nada, Nadia.

NAHAMA (Hebrew) 'comfort from God'. Var. and dim., Nahaman, Nahamas, Ama, Hama, Naham.

NAN, NANCY see **ANN.**

NANETTE, NINON see **ANN.**

NAOMI (Hebrew. Pron: nayomi) 'sweet, pleasant'. Dim., Nomi.

NARDA (origin uncertain) 'joyous, gay'. Var., Nara.

NATALIE (Latin) 'Christmas child'. A feminine of Nathan. Var. and dim., Natala, Natale, Natalee, Natalia, Natasha, Nathalie, Natica, Natika, Nat, Nattie, Netta, Nettie, Netty.

NEDA (Slavonic) 'Sunday's child'. Var. and dim., Nedda, Ned, Nedi, Neddy.

NELDA (Old English) 'of the elder tree'. Var. and dim., Nellda, Elda, Nell, Nelly.

NELL, NELLA, N LLIE, NELLY see **CORNELIA, HELEN.**

NEOMA (Greek. Pron: neeoma) 'light of the new moon'.

Var. and dim., Neomah, Neeoma, Nea, Neo, Neom.

NEOTA (Old English. Pron: neeota) 'compulsion'.

NERINE (Greek) 'sea nymph'. Var. and dim., Nereen, Nerin, Neri.

NERISSA (Greek) 'of the sea'. Var., Nerita.

NESTA Welsh diminutive for Agnes. Var., Nessie.

NETTA, NETTIE Scottish diminutive of Janet.

NEULA (Pron: noola) maybe Celtic 'champion'.

NEYSA (Greek) 'pure'. Var. and dim., Neisa, Nisa, Nysa, see also **AGNES**.

NICOLE (Greek) 'victory of the people'. Feminine of Nicholas. Var. and dim., Nichola, Nicola, Nicolette, Nikola, Niki, Nikki.

NINA Russian diminutive of Anne occasionally used in the British Isles.

NIOBE (Greek. Pron: niobi) The name of the Queen of Thebes punished by the goddess Leto for her pride.

NITA Spanish abbreviation of Juanita – (Joan).

NOEL (Latin) 'born on Christmas Day'. Feminine of Noel. Var., Noella, Noelle.

NOLA (Celtic) 'famous, wellknown'. Feminine of Nolan.

NOLITA (Latin) 'olive groves'. Var. and dim., Nolitta, Lita, Noli.

NONA (Latin) 'ninth born'. Var. and dim., Nonah, Nonna, Nonny, Anona.

NONIE pet form of Norah.

NORA, NORAH Irish abbreviation of Honoria.

NOREEN, NORLEEN, NORINE, NORRIE Irish diminutives of Nora.

NORMA (Latin) maybe 'pattern', 'model', 'rule'. Feminine of Norman. Dim., Normi, Normie.

O

OCTAVIA (Latin) 'the eighth born'. Feminine of Octavius. Dim., Tavia, Tavi, Ottavia.

ODELE (Greek) 'a melody'. Var., Odel, Odelet, Odell.

ODELIA (Old German) 'prosperous'. Var., Odella.

ODETTE (French from old German) 'fatherland'. Var., Odet, Odetta.

OLA (Scandinavian) 'daughter or descendant'. The feminine of Olaf.

OLETHEA (Latin. Pron: oleethia) 'truth'. Var. and dim., Alethea, Oletha, Aletha, Thea.

OLGA (Russian, from Norse) 'holy'.

OLINDA maybe from the Russian 'holy'.

OLIVIA (Latin) 'olive tree'. Feminine of Oliver. Var. and dim., Olive, Livi, Livia, Livvi, Olli, Ollie.

OLWEN (Welsh) 'white track' (of flowers). Var., Olwin.

ONA, OONAH see **UNA**.

OPAL (Sanskrit) 'jewel'.

OPHELIA (Greek) 'help', 'succour'. Dim., Phelia.

ORA, ORALIA, ORALIE, OREL see **AURELIA**.

ORINTHIA Invented by Shaw for the king's lady in *The Apple-cart*, and sometimes used as a Christian name since.

ORIOLE (Old German) 'fire', 'strife'. Var., Auriol.

ORLENA (Latin) 'golden'. Var., Orlene, Orlina.

ORNA (Irish) 'olive-coloured'. Var., Ornam, Ornas.

ORVA (Old English) 'the brave friend'. Var. and dim., Orvam, Orvas, Orv.

OTTILIE (Old German) 'fatherland'. Var. and dim., Otila, Otillia, Otti, Ottie.

P

PAMELA The name of a character in Sir Philip Sydney's *Arcadia* which was then borrowed by a novelist who made it popular.

PANDORA (Greek) 'talented; gifted'. Dim., Dora, Dorie.

PANSY (Greek) The name of the flower (found often in Cornwall). Var., Pansie.

PAT see **PATRICIA**.

PATIENCE (Latin) 'patient'. Dim., Patty.

PATRICIA (Latin) 'nobility; well born'. Feminine of Patrick. Var. and dim., Patrice, Pat, Patsy, Patti.

PATTY (Hebrew) 'becoming bitter'.

PAULA (Latin) 'little'. Feminine of Paul. Var. and dim., Paola, Paulette, Paulina, Pauline, Paulita, Pauli, Paulie, Pol, Polly.

PAULINE, PAULINA see **PAULA**.

PEACE (English) 'peace'.

PEARL (English) used in modern times as a Christian name as Ruby, Emerald, etc. Var. and dim., Pearle, Perle, Perl, Perlie.

PEG, PEGGY see **MARGARET**.

PEGA (Greek) 'joined together'. Var., Pegma.

PEGEEN (Irish) 'pearl'.

PENELOPE (Greek) 'weaver'. Dim., Pen, Pennie, Penny.

PENTECOST (Greek) 'fiftieth day'. Sometimes used for children born at Whitsuntide.

PEONY (Greek) 'flower'. Var. and dim., Peonie, Ony.

PEPITA (Spanish) 'she shall add'. Dim., Pepi, Peta.

PERDITA (Latin) 'lost'. A name invented by Shakespeare for the lost child in *A Winter's Tale*.

PERNEL (English) 'stone'.

41

PERPETUA (Latin) 'everlasting'. Var. and dim., Perpetuam, Perpetuas, Perpett, Petta, Petua.

PERSEPHONE (Greek) The name of the goddess of spring.

PERSIS (Greek) 'Persian woman'. Var., Persas.

PETALIA (English) 'flower petal'. Dim., Petal.

PETRA see **PETRINA**.

PETRINA (Greek) 'steadfast; resolute'. Feminine of Peter. Var. and dim., Petra, Petrine, Peti, Petie, Trina.

PETRONELLA (Latin.) The feminine of Petronius possibly 'stone'. Var. and dim., Petronilla, Pernel, Parnel.

PETULA (English) A modern name, meaning uncertain.

PETUNIA (English) The name of the flower sometimes used as a Christian name in recent times.

PHENICE (Hebrew) 'from a palm tree'. Var. and dim., Phenica, Venice, Pheni.

PHILIPPA (Greek) 'lover of horses'. Feminine of Philip. Var. and dim., Philippa, Philippe, Pippa.

PHILLIDA (Greek) 'leafy'. Var. and dim., Phillada, Villada, Phyllis, Phyllissa, Phyl, Felice.

PHILOMENA (Greek. Pron: filomeena) 'loving thought'. Dim., Mena.

PHOEBE (Greek. Pron: feebi) 'shining'. Var., Phebe.

PHYLLIS see **PHILLIDA**.

PIA (Italian. Pron: peea) 'devout'.

PIPPA see **PHILIPPA**.

POLLY see **MARY**.

POMONA (Latin. Pron: pomona) 'fertile'. Var., Pamona.

POPPY (Latin) The name of the scarlet flower. Var., Poppi.

PORTIA (Latin. Pron: Porshia) of uncertain meaning.

PRAGNA (Latin) maybe a feminization of Pragmatius, a 6th-century saint.

PRIAULX (Pron: preeo) An African name, meaning uncertain.

PRIMA (Latin. Pron: preema) 'first born'. Var., Prema.

PRIMROSE (Latin) 'the first rose'. Dim., Rose, Rosie.

PRIMULA (Latin) 'cowslip'.

PRISCILLA (Latin) Feminine diminutive of Priscus 'former'. Var. and dim., Prisilla, Pris, Prissie, Prissy, Sil.

PROTASIA (Latin. Pron: protayzia) Feminine of Protasius. Of uncertain meaning.

PRUDENCE (Latin) 'prudent', 'cautious'. Dim., Pru, Prud, Prudi, Prudie, Prudy.

PRUNELLA The Latin name for the 'self heal' plant.

Q

QUEENIE (English) A pet name which became a name in its own right. Var., Queena, Queeny.

QUENBY (Scandinavian) 'wife; womanly'.

QUERIDA (Spanish) 'loved one'. Var. and dim., Queridas, Queridis, Querius, Queri, Erida, Rida.

R

RACHEL (Hebrew) 'ewe' 'lamb'. Var. and dim., Rachele, Rachelle, Rochelle, Rae, Ray, Shelley.

RAMONA (Old German) 'protector'. Feminine of Raymond. Dim., Mona, Rama.

RANA (Sanskrit) 'of royalty'. Var. and dim., Rania, Rani.

RAQUEL (Indian) meaning uncertain.

REBECCA (Hebrew) possibly 'heifer'. Var., Rebekah, Reba, Riba, Riva, Becky.

REGINA (Latin) 'Queen'. Var. and dim., Regan, Regine, Gina, Gine, Reggie.

RENEE (French. Pron: renay) 'reborn'. Var. and dim., Renata, Reni, Renne.

RENITA (Latin) 'confident'. Var. and dim., Ranita, Raniti, Reneta, Reniti, Nita, Rani, Reni, Riti.

REZARE (Cornish. Pron: rezari) 'water crossing'.

RHEA (Greek) 'motherly'.

RHODA (Greek) 'rose'. Var. and dim., Rhodah, Rhonda, Rodi, Rodie.

RHONA see **ROANNA.**

RICARDA (Old German) 'ruler'. Var. and dim., Ricardama, Ricardas, Richenda, Richenza, Ric, Rica.

RICHENDA, RICHENZA see **RICARDA.**

RITA (Greek) 'a pearl'. A dim. of Norita, Margarita, Clarita, etc. but used also as a name in its own right.

ROANNA (Latin) 'sweet; gracious'. Var. and dim., Roana, Rona, Anna, Rhona.

ROBERTA (Old English) 'bright fame'. Feminine of Robert. Var. and dim., Robina, Ruberta, Ruperta, Bobbe, Bobbi, Bobbie, Robin, Robinette, Robi, Robbi, Robbie.

ROCANA (Old German) meaning uncertain.

ROCHELLE see **RACHEL.**

RODERICA (Old German) 'fame'; 'rule'. Feminine of Roderick. Var. and dim., Roderika, Rodrica, Rica.

ROESIA (English) 'fame'.

ROLANDA (Old German) 'famed land'. Feminine of Roland. Dim., Ro, Rola.

ROMA (Latin) from the name of the city of Rome. Var., Romaine.

ROMOLA Italian feminine of Latin Romulus who gave his name to the city of Rome. Var. and dim., Romolas, Mola, Romo, Romoa, Romy.

RONALDA (Old German) 'powerful'. Feminine of Ronald. Dim., Ronnie, Ronny.

RONAT (Celtic) 'seal'.

ROSABEL (Latin) 'beautiful rose'. Var. and dim., Rosabella, Rosabelle, Rosa, Belle.

ROSALBA (Latin) 'white rose'. Var. and dim., Roselba, Rosellba, Alba, Rosaba, Salba, Sallba.

ROSALIE (Latin) The name of the ceremony of hanging garlands of roses on tombs.

ROSALIND (Old German) a compound of 'horse' and 'serpent'. Var. and dim., Rosalinde, Roselyn, Roslyn, Rosalyn, Ros, Roz.

ROSE (Latin) 'a rose', but may also be a derivative of Old German 'horse' as in Rosalind. Var. and dim., Rosa, Rosalee, Rosaleen, Rosalia, Rosalie, Rosamond, Rosamund, Rosena, Rosene, Rosel, Rosella, Roselle, Rosette, Rosina, Rizona, Rozalie, Rosi, Rosie, Rosy.

ROSEANNA An 18th-century mixing of Rose and Anna. Var., Roseanne.

ROSEMARY 18th-century mixing of Rose and Mary. Var. and dim., Rosemare, Rosemari, Rosemarie.

ROSETTA 18th-century diminutive of Rose.

ROWENA probably Old English 'famed friend'.

ROXANE (Persian) 'dawn'. Var., Roxana, Roxanna, Roxanne, Rox, Roxie, Roxy.

RUBY (English) The name of the precious stone. Var., Rubetta.

RUFINA (Latin. Pron: roofeena) 'red' (haired). Var. and dim., Rufena, Ruffina, Ruphina, Fina, Rufi.

RUPERTA (Old German) 'bright fame'. Feminine of Rupert.

RUTH (Hebrew) 'beauty'. Var. and dim., Ruthia, Ruthi, Ruthie.

S

SABINA (Latin) 'Sabine woman'. Var. and dim., Sabin, Savina, Bina.

SABRINA (Old English) 'The river Severn', or 'a princess'. Dim., Brina.

SACHA (Greek) 'helpmate'.

SADIE, SADYE see SARAH.

SADIRA (Arabic. Pron: Sadeera) 'from the water'. Var. and dim., Sadirah, Sadiras, Dira.

SALEMA (Hebrew) 'peace'. Var. and dim., Selemas, Selima, Lima.

SALENA (Greek. Pron: saleena) 'salty'. Var. and dim., Salina, Sal, Sale, Sali.

SALLIE, SALLY (Hebrew) 'princess'.

SALOME (Aramaic) 'peace of Zion'. Var. and dim., Sallome, Saloma, Salomie, Sal, Sale, Salo.

SAMALA (Hebrew. Pron: samahla) 'prayed for'. Var. and dim., Samalam, Samalas, Samal, Sam, Sama, Sammy.

SAMANTHA (American Indian) 'lovely flower'. Var. and dim., Samanthia, Sama, Sam.

SAMARA (Hebrew) 'watchful; cautious'. Dim., Mara.

SAMUELA (Hebrew) 'name of God'. Feminine of Samuel. Var. and dim., Samuella, Ela, Sam, Uela.

SANDRA Italian abbreviation of Allesandra (Alexandra), now a name in its own right.

SAPPHIRA (Hebrew) The name of the precious blue stone. Var. and dim., Sapphera, Fira, Phira.

SARAH (Hebrew) 'princess'. Var. and dim., Sadye, Sara, Sarena, Sarene, Saretta, Sharon, Sari, Shari, Sarita, Shirin, Sadie, Sadye, Sal, Sallie, Sally.

SECUNDA (Latin) 'second born'. Var., Secundas.

SELA (Hebrew) 'a rock'. Var., Saleta, Sella.

SELINA (probably French from Latin) 'heaven'. Var. and dim., Selena, Zelina, Lina, Lena.

SELINDA (Old German) 'conquering snake'.

SELMA (Scottish) 'fair'.

SENALDA (Spanish) 'sign; omen'. Var. and dim., Sanalda, Sanald, Senald, Alda, Enalda, Sena.

SEPTIMA (Latin) 'seventh'. Var. and dim., Septimas, Tima.

SERENA (Latin) 'tranquil'. 'serene'. Var., Serina.

SERILDA (Old German) 'girl of war'. Var. and dim., Sarilda, Sorilda, Rilda.

SETHRIDA (Latin) 'appointed by the Lord'. Dim., Seth, Thrida.

SHAMA (Hebrew) 'obedient woman'. Var., Shemma.

SHARON see **SARAH**.

SHEBA (Pron: sheeba) see **BATHSHEBA**.

SHEENA English way of pronouncing the Gaelic Sine (Jane).

SHEILA English way of pronouncing the Irish Sile (Celia). Var. and dim., Shela, Shelah, Sheys, Shelley.

SHERYL, SHERRY, SHERI see **SHIRLEY**.

SHIMONA (Hebrew) 'little princess'.

SHIRIN A form of Sharon.

SHIRLEY An Old English surname. Var. and dim., Sheryl, Shirlee, Sherry, Sheri, Shirl, Shirlie.

SHONET (Celtic) maybe 'sower'.

SIDONY (Latin) 'fine cloth', 'linen'.

SIDWELL (English) Name taken from St. Satirola, who was martyred in Devon.

SIMONE (Hebrew) 'obedient'. Feminine of Simon. Var., Simonetta.

SIRI (Norman) 'conquering impulse'.

SOLITA (Latin) 'standard setter'. Var. and dim., Solitta, Lita, Sola.

SONDRA see **ALEXANDRA**.

SONIA Russian diminutive of Sophia.

SOPHIA (Greek. Pron: sofia) 'wisdom'. Var. and dim., Sofia, Sonia, Sonja, Senya, Soph, Sophi, Sophie, Sophey, Sophy.

SOPHRONIA (Greek. Pron: sofronia) 'of sound mind'.

SORRELL (English) The name of the russet flowered plant, sometimes used as a Christian name in recent times.

STACEY see **ANASTASIA**.

STELLA (Latin) 'star'.

STEPHANIE (French from Greek) 'crown'. Feminine of Stephen. Var. and dim., Stefanie, Stephana, Stephania, Stephenie, Stevie.

STEWARTINA (Scottish) Feminine of Stewart, the name of the royal clan.

SUSAN (Hebrew) 'lilly'. Var. and dim., Susana, Susanna, Susanne, Susannah, Suzanna, Sue, Susi, Susie, Susy, Suzie, Suzy, Suki, Susa.

SYBIL (Greek) 'the prophetess'. Var. and dim., Sibel, Sibell, Sibyl, Sybyl, Sib, Sibie, Sibbie, Sibby.

SYDEL (Hebrew) 'the enchantress'. Var., Sydelle.

SYDNEY (French) Family name taken from St. Denis. Feminine of Sidney. Var. and dim., Sidney, Sidonia, Sid, Syd.

SIGRID (Old Norse) 'victory'.

SYLVIA (Latin) 'wood'. Var. and dim., Silva, Silvana, Silvia, Syl, Sylvie.

T

TABITHA (Aramaic) 'gazelle'. Dim., Tabbie, Tabby.

TACE, TAYCE (English) 'be silent'.

TAGGET see **AGNES**.

TALITHA (Aramaic) 'damsel arise'. Var. and dim., Talita, Telita, Telitha, Litha, Lita, Talith.

TALLULAH A modern American name. Var. and dim., Tallula, Tallu.

TAMAR (English. Pron: taymah) 'palm'.

TAMARA A Russian Hebrew name now sometimes used in the British Isles. Possibly, 'palm tree'.

TAMSIN, TAMASINE see THOMASINA.

TAMARISK (Latin) The name of the pink flowering tree.

TANIA see TATIANA.

TARA (Celtic) 'tower'.

TERESA (Greek) 'carrying ears of corn'. Var. and dim., Theresa, Therese, Tracey, Tracy, Tess, Tessa, Tessie.

TERTIA (Latin: Pron: tershia) 'the third child'. Var. and dim., Tertiam, Tertias, Tertium, Teria, Terti, Tia.

TERZA (Greek) 'pleasantness'. Var. and dim., Terzam, Terzas, Terrzam, Terrzas, Tera, Terr.

TESSA, TESS Abbreviation of Teresa, which became popular after Thomas Hardy's novel *Tess of the Durbevilles*.

THALIA (Greek. Pron: thahlia) 'blooming'. Var., Thalea.

THEA, THEDA see THEODORA.

THELMA (Greek) 'nursing'.

THEODORA (Greek) 'God's gift'. The feminine of Theodor. Var. and dim., Dora, Dori, Teddi, Teddie, Theda, Thea, Theo.

THEODOSIA (Greek) 'divine gift'.

THEOLA (Greek) 'heavensent'. Dim., Lola, Theo.

THEONE (Greek) 'godly'.

THEOPHANIA (Greek) 'manifestation of God'. Dim., Tiffany.

THERA (Greek) 'untamed'.

THETIS (Greek. Pron: theetis) 'beautiful nymph of the sea; the sea goddess'. Var. and dim., Thetas, Thetes, Thetisa, Thetos, Thetus, Heti.

THOMASINA (Aramaic) 'the twin'. Feminine of Thomas. Var. and dim., Tamsin, Tamasin, Thomasa, Thomasine.

THORA (Norwegian) 'thunder'.

TIANA see GRATIANA.

TIBBY see ELIZABETH.

TIBELDA (English) 'people's prince'.

TIFFANY see THEOPHANIA.

TILDA, TILLIE, TILLY see MATHILDA.

TIMOTHEA (Greek) 'honouring God'. Feminine of Timothy. Dim., Thea, Tim, Timmie.

TIRZAH see THIRZA.

TINA see CHRISTINE, ERNESTINE, MARTINA.

TONI see ANTONIA.

TRACY see TERESA.

TRILBY (Scandinavian) 'frivolous; giddy'. Var. and dim., Trilbee, Trilbi, Trillbee, Trillbi, Trillby, Trie, Triley, Trill, Trilly, Trilli.

TRINA (Greek) 'pure'. Var. and dim., Trinas, Trinee, Trini, Trinia, Treen, Tri, Trin.

TRINETTE (Greek) 'purity'. Var. and dim., Trinetta, Rinee, Trini, Triny.

TRISTA (Latin) 'woman of much sadness'. Var. and dim., Tristas, Tristis, Tristus, Tristusa, Tris.

TRIXIE see **BEATRICE**.

TRUDY see **GERTRUDE**.

U

UDELE (Old English. Pron: yudeyli) 'great wealth'. Var. and dim., Udela, Udelas, Udeles, Udella, Udelle, Udellas, Udelles, Delle, Uda.

ULA (Celtic) 'see jewel'.

ULLA (Norwegian. Pron: ulla) 'will'. Var. and dim., Ula, Ullah, Ylla, Ule, Yle.

UNA (Latin) 'one'. Var., Ona, Oonagh.

UNDINE (Latin) 'of water'. Var., Undene.

UNIS see **EUNICE**.

URSA (Greek) 'nymph of the sky; she-bear'. Var. and dim., Ursal, Ursala, Ursam, Ursas, Yursa, Yursal, Yursam, Urs, Yurs.

URSULA (Latin) 'she-bear'. Var. and dim., Ursa, Ursel, Ursulette, Ursi.

V

VALDA (Old German) 'battle heroine'. Dim., Val.

VALEDA (Old German) 'wholesome'. Var. and dim., Valedas, Valeta, Valetas, Aleda, Aledas, Leda, Vala, Vale.

VALENTINA (Latin) 'strong' 'healthy'. Feminine of Valentine. Var. and dim., Valencia, Valentia, Valerie, Valeria, Valora, Val, Vallie.

VALERIE (Latin) The feminine of Valerius, the name of a Roman family. Var., Valeria.

VALONIA (Latin) 'from the far valley' Var. and dim., Valoniah, Valonnia, Vallonia, Valloniah, Val.

VANDA see **WANDA**.

VANESSA Invented by Swift for *Cadmus and Vanessa*, and since adopted more generally. Var. and dim., Vanesa, Vanni, Van.

VANORA (Scottish) 'white wave'.

VEDA (Sanskrit) 'wise'. Var., Veeda, Vedah, Vedda.

VEDIS (Old German) 'wood or forest spirit'. Var. and dim., Veedis, Vedus, Vedi.

VELDA (Old German) 'wise woman'. Var., Valeda.

VELMA see **WILHELMINA**.

VENTIA A Latinization of the Welsh Gwyneth, 'white brow'. Var., Venora.

VERA (Russian) 'faith'.

VERADA (Latin) 'genuine; forthright'. Var. and dim., Veradas, Veradia, Veredes, Veredos, Veredus, Eradis, Vera, Veradi.

VERDA (Latin) 'blooming'. Dim., Verdie.

VERENA probably Old German, 'folk'. Var., Verona, Verinia.

VERITY (English) an abstract noun which came into use in the 17th century.

VERNA (Latin) 'spring-born'. Feminine of Vernon. Var., Vernice, Vernita.

VERONICA (Latin) 'image'. Var., Ronnie, Tonny.

VICTORIA (Latin) 'victory'. Feminine of Victor. Var. and dim., Victorie, Victorine, Vicki, Vicky.

VIDA (Hebrew) 'beloved'. Var., Vidda, Viddah.

VINNA (Old English) 'of the vine'. Var., Vina, Vinella.

VIOLA (Latin. Pron: viola) 'violet'.

VIOLET (Old French, diminutive of Latin Viola). Var. and dim., Viola, Violetta, Violette, Vi.

VIRGINIA (Latin) feminine of Virginius, the name of a Roman family. Var. and dim., Virgilia, Virginie, Ginger, Ginny, Jinny, Vlrg, Virgy.

VIRTUE (English) Abstract noun used as a Christian name in the 18th century and sometimes since.

VITA (Latin) 'life; vital'. Feminine of Vito.

VIVIEN (Latin) 'lively; full of life'. Var. and dim., Viviane, Vivienne, Vi, Viv, Vivi, Vivia, Vivie.

W

WANDA (Old German) maybe stem; 'slender'. Var., Wenda, Vanda.

WENDY see **GWENDOLEN**.

WESLA (Old English) 'from the West meadow'. Var. and dim., Wesle, Weslee, Wesleed, Wes, Wesa.

WILFREDA (Old German) 'firm peacemaker'. Feminine of Wilfred. Dim., Freda.

WILHELMINA (Old German) 'will' 'helmet'. Feminine of Wilhelm. Var. and dim., Velma, Wilma, Mina.

WILLA (Old English) 'desirable'. Feminine of William. Var. and dim., Wila, Willy.

WILLOW (English) The name of the tree sometimes used as a Christian name.

WINIFRED (Old German) 'friend of peace'. Var. and dim., Winny, Freda.

WINONA (Pron: winona) see **WENONA**.

WIRA (Celtic. Pron: wira) 'gentlewoman of the castle'. Var. and dim., Wera, Werra, Wirra, Irra, Weer, Wir.

WIVINIA (Latin) 'of the quiet life'. Var. and dim., Wivina, Wiviniah, Wivvinnia, Vinia, Wivina.

WYNNE (Celtic) 'the fair or the white'. Var., Wyne.

X

XANTHE (Greek) 'blonde'.
XENA (Greek) 'hospitable'. Var., Xenia, Zenia.
XYLIA (Greek) 'of the wood'.

Y

YASMINE see JASMINE.
YEDA (Hebrew. Pron: yeyda) 'heart's ease'.
YETTA (Hebrew) 'mistress of the house'. Var. and dim., Yeta, Yetah, Yettah, Yetti.
YOLANDE Mediaeval French form of the Latin Violante, 'violet'. Var., Yolanda.
YSEULTE (Celtic. Pron: eezult) 'girl of white skin'. Var. and dim., Yseulta, Yseulti, Seulta, Seulte, Yseult.
YVELINE Pet form of Eve.
YVONNE (Old French) 'yew tree'. Var. and dim., Ivonne, Yvette, Von, Vonnie.

Z

ZABRINA (Old English) 'of the nobility'. Var. and dim., Zabrine, Brina.
ZADIA (Greek) 'fair minded'.

ZALEHKA (Hebrew) meaning uncertain.
ZAMORA (Spanish) 'from the hills'. Var. and dim., Zamoras, Zammora, Amora, Zam, Zama, Zamo.
ZANDRA (Greek) 'friend' or 'helper of mankind'.
ZEBALDA (Hebrew) 'gift of the Lord'. Feminine of Zebadiah. Dim., Zeba.
ZELAH Cornish place name.
ZELATA (Hebrew. Pron: zelahta). Var., Zlata.
ZELDA see GRISELDA.
ZELIDE (Hebrew) 'heaven sent'.
ZELINA see SELINA.
ZENA (Greek) 'hospitable'. Var., Zeena, Zenia.
ZENAIDA (Hebrew) 'mountain goat'.
ZENKA (Slavonic) 'ice glade'.
ZENOBIA (Aramaic) 'father's ornament'. Var., Zenovia.
ZERLINA (Old German) 'serene and beautiful'. Var. and dim., Zerline, Zerla.
ZILLAH (Hebrew) 'shade'.
ZINEVRA (Celtic) 'white wave'.
ZITA (Celtic) 'enticing'. Var. and dim., Zitah, Zitta, Ita, Zi.
ZIVANA (Slavonic) 'living'.
ZOBA (Old German) 'daughter of the ruler'. Var. and dim., Zobba, Zobe, Zoe.
ZOE (Greek) 'life'.

ZOHELETHA (Hebrew. Pron: zoeletha) 'serpent stone'. Var. and dim., Zoheleetha, Zohelletha, Zoheleth, Zohell.

ZORA (Latin) 'dawn'. Var., Zorah, Zorana, Zorina.

ZOSIMA (Greek) 'riches'. Var. and dim., Zoseema, Zoseemah, Zosimah, Sima, Zosi, Zossi.

ZULEIKA (Arabic. Pron: zulika). 'fair'.

NAMES FOR BOYS

A

AARON (Hebrew. Pron: Airon) 'light; high mountain'. Var., Aron, Aharon.

ABEL (Hebrew. Pron: Aybel) 'Breath'.

ABELARD (Old German. Pron: Abelard) 'Noble; firm'.

ABRAHAM (Hebrew. Pron: Aybraham) 'Father of nations'. Var. and dim., Abram, Arram, Abe, Abie, Bram.

ABSALOM (Hebrew. Pron: Absalom) 'God is peace'.

ACHILLES (Greek. Pron: Akilleez) 'swift, lipless'.

ACKERLEY (Old English) 'from the meadow of the oak trees'.

ADAIR (Celtic. Pron: Adair) possibly 'from the oak tree ford'.

ADALARD (Old German) 'Noble eagle'.

ADAM (Hebrew) 'red earth' (out of which it is said God formed him). Var., Addam.

ADDISON (Old English) 'Adam's descendant'.

ADIN (Hebrew. Pron: Aydin) 'voluptuous; sensual'. Var., Adan.

ADLEY (Hebrew) 'the fair minded'. Var., Adalon, Adlay, Adlee, Adlei.

ADRIAN (Latin. Pron: Aydrian) 'of the Adriatic'.

ADRIEL (Hebrew) 'from the Lord's kingdom'. Var., Adrial, Adriell, Adrell, Adiel.

AENEAS (Greek. Pron: Aneeas) 'worthy of praise'.

AIDAN (Celtic) 'firey'. Var., Aedan.

AINSLEY (Old English) 'from the near field'. Var., Ainslie, Ainsworth.

AJAX (Greek) 'earthy'.

AKAN (Egyptian. Pron: Aykan) 'migrant people'.

ALAN (Celtic) 'harmony'. Var., Alain, Allan, Alein, Alun.

ALARD (Old German) 'noble-hard'.

ALARIC (Old German) 'wolf ruler'. Var. and dim., Alarick, Alberic, Ullric, Ulrich, Ulrick, Rick.

ALASTAIR see **ALEXANDER**.

ALBERT (Old German) 'noble and bright'. Var. and dim., Adalbert, Delbert, Elbert, Ethelbert, Al, Bert, Bertie.

ALDEN (Old English. Pron: Awlden) 'old friend'. Var. and dim., Aldin, Aldwin, Alwin, Al.

ALDO (Old German) 'great'.

ALDOUS (Old German. Pron: Awldous) 'great; wise'. Var., Aldis, Aldus.

ALEX Alick (Scottish) dim. of Alexander.

ALEXANDER (Greek) 'protector of men'. Var. and dim., Alastair, Allister, Sanders, Sandor, Saunders, Al, Alec, Aleck, Alex, Alexis, Alick, Sandy.

ALEXIS (Greek) 'defender'.

ALFIE see **ALFRED**.

ALFRED (Old English) 'Elf counsel'. Var. and dim., Al, Alf, Alfie, Alfy.

ALLISTER see **ALEXANDER.**

ALOYSIUS (French) 'famous battle'.

ALPHEUS (Greek) the name of a 4th-century saint martyred under Diocletian.

ALROY (Latin) 'the king'.

ALSTONE (Old English) 'noble stone'.

ALTON (Old English) 'ancient village'.

ALVAR (Old English) 'elf army'.

ALVERY (French from Old English) 'Elf counsel'. The French form of Alfred.

ALVIN (Old German) 'noble friend'. Var., Alvan, Alwin, Alwyn, Elvin.

AMADIS (French–Latin) 'Love of God'.

AMBLER (Old English) 'keeper of horses'. Var., Ambrey.

AMBROSE (Latin) 'immortal'.

AMIEL (Hebrew. Pron: Amyel) 'of the land'.

AMORY (Latin) 'loving'. Var., Amery, Amary.

AMOS (Hebrew) 'carried by God'.

AMSDEN (Old English) possibly 'from the valley'.

AMYOT (English diminutive of Latin or Old French name Ame. Pron: Amiō) Var., Amyas, Aimo, Aaymo.

ANANIAS (Hebrew) 'Grace of the Lord'.

ANATOL (Greek. Pron: Anatol) 'of the East'. Var., Anatole.

ANDREW (Greek) 'manly'. Var. and dim., Anders, Andy, Andreas, Andrien.

ANEURIN (Welsh–Latin) 'honoured'; old spelling Aneirin.

ANGUS (Scottish) 'chosen one'. Dim., Gus.

ANSTY (Greek. Pron: Ansti) 'resurrection'. Var., Anstey.

ANTON A German form of **ANTHONY.**

ANTHONY (Latin–English) 'Inestimable'. Var. and dim., Antoine, Antoni, Antony, Tony.

ANTIMUS (Latin) 'beyond praise'.

AQUILLA (Latin–English. Pron: Akwilla) 'eagle'.

ARCHIE (Old German) 'truly bold'.

ARDELL (Old English) 'of the dell'. Var., Ardel.

ARDEN (Latin) 'fervent; eager and sincere'.

ARGENT (French) 'silver'.

ARGYLE (Celtic) 'belonging to Ireland'. Var., Argile, Argille, Argylle.

ARKWRIGHT (Old English) 'carpenter'. Var. and dim., Arkwhite, Arkwhit, Wright.

ARMAND, ARMIN, AR-MOND see HERMAN.

ARMSTRONG (Old English) 'with a strong arm'.

ARNOLD (Old German) 'powerful as an eagle'. Dim., Arne, Arnie, Arno.

ARTHUR (Latin) 'strong as a bear'. Var. and dim., Aurthur, Arturo, Art, Artie.

ARUNDELL (Old English) 'of the dell of eagles'. Var., Arondell, Arondel, Arundel.

ARVELL (Celtic) 'cried for'.

ARVIN (Old German) 'a friend of the people'. Dim., Ari, Arnie, Arvy.

ASHER (Hebrew) 'fortunate'.

ASHLEY (Old English) 'from the field of the ash trees'. Dim., Lee.

AUBIN (Latin) 'fair; white'. Var., Albion.

AUBREY (Old German) 'elf ruler'. Dim., Bree, Brey.

AUDLEY (Old English) 'prospering'. Var., Audley.

AUGUSTIN (Latin) 'consecrated, venerated'. Var., Augustine.

AUGUSTUS (Latin) 'exalted'. Var. and dim., August, Gustin, Augie, Gus.

AULAY (Gaelic, Scandinavian) a form of Olaf. 'Carrier of tradition'.

AURE dim. of AURELIUS.

AURELIUS (Latin) 'golden friend'. Var., Aretus.

AURIN (Welsh) 'gold'.

AUSTIN (Latin) 'venerated, consecrated'. Var., Austen.

AVERY (Old English. Pron: Ayveri) 'Ruler of the elves'.

AVENEL (Old German) 'battle with the beasts'.

AXEL (Scandinavian) 'divine reward'.

AYLMER (Old English) 'noble and famous'.

AYLWYN, ALWYN (Old German) 'noble friend'.

AYMARD (Old English) 'work ruler'.

AYMON (Old French–Germanic) 'home loving'.

B

BAILEY (Teutonic) 'able'.

BALFORE (Gaelic) 'from the meadow'. Var. and dim., Balfour, Balf, Bal.

BALLARD (Latin) probably 'babbler'.

BALTHASAR (Persian) 'war counsel'.

BANCROFT (Old English) 'from the bean field'.

BANQUO (Gaelic) 'white, fair'.

BARCLAY see BERKELEY.

BARDEN (Old English) 'he who lives near the boar's den'. Var., Borden.

BARDOLPH (Old English) 'bright wolf'.

BARLOW (Old English) 'he lives on the boar's hill'. Var., Borlow.

BARNABY (Hebrew) 'son of consolation'. Var. and dim., Barnabas, Barney.

BARNARD, BARNET, BARNETT see BERNARD.

BARNEY see BARNABY, BERNARD.

BARRET (Old German) 'mighty as a bear'. Var., Barrett.

BARRON (Old English) 'of noble blood'. Var. and dim., Baron, Barren, Barr.

BARRY (Celtic) 'spear'.

BARTHOLOMEW (Hebrew) 'son of a thousand furrows'; from 'Son of Talmai' (abounding in furrows). Var. and dim., Bardo, Barth, Barthol, Bartley, Bart, Bat, Bartie.

BARTLETT (Hebrew) 'son of the furrows'.

BARTON (Old English) 'farmer'. Dim., Bart, Barth.

BASIL (Greek. Pron: Bazil) 'kingly'.

BAXTER (Old German) 'the baker'. Dim., Bac.

BAYAARD (French. Pron: Bayard) 'of the fiery hair; redhead'. Var., Baird.

BEAUFORT (French. Pron: Bofort) 'of the huge fortress'. Var., Beaufert, Beaufurt.

BEAVIS (Old English–French. Pron: Beevis) 'strong as an ox'.

BEDIVERE (English, Welsh) 'birch hero'. Var., Bedver.

BELAMY (French) 'beautiful friend'. Var., Bellamy.

BELDEN (Old German) 'from a beautiful valley'.

BEN, BENNY see BENEDICT, BENJAMIN, BENTON.

BENEDICT (Latin) 'blessed'. Var. and dim., Benedic, Benedick, Benedix, Bennet, Bennett, Ben, Benny, Dixon.

BENIAH (Hebrew. Pron: Beniah) 'son of the Lord'.

BENJAMIN (Hebrew) literally 'son of the south'. (Son of my right hand). Var. and dim., Benson, Ben, Benjie, Benjy, Bennie, Benny.

BENNETT see BENEDICT.

BENTON (Old English) 'of the moors'. Dim., Ben.

BERENGER (Old German) 'the spearer of boars'. Var., Beringer, Benger.

BERKELEY (Old English. Pron: Bahkli) 'from the birch meadow'. Var., Barclay, Berkley.

BERNARD (Old German) 'Strong as a bear'. Var. and dim., Barnard, Barnet, Barnett, Bernarr, Bernhard, Barney, Bern, Bernie, Barend.

BERT see ALBERT, BERTRAM, HERBERT.

BERTRAM (Latin) 'bright raven'. Var. and dim., Bartram, Bert, Bertie, Bertrand.

BERWICK (Old German. Pron: Berrik) 'from the barley fields'.

BERTWIN (Old English) 'illustrious friend'.

BETHAN (Welsh. Pron: Bethan) 'life'.

BEVAN (Celtic. Pron: Bevan) 'the son of the young warrior'. Var., Bevin.

BEVERLEY (Old English. Pron: Beverli) 'from the beaver meadow'.

BEVIS (Old English) thought to mean 'beautiful one'. Var., Bobo.

BILL see **WILLIAM**.

BIRON Surname sometimes used as Christian name. The most famous bearer being the poet Byron. Var., Byron.

BLAIN (French) probably 'white-fair'.

BLAIR (Celtic) 'a place'.

BLAKE Surname sometimes used as Christian name, the most illustrious bearer being the poet William Blake.

BLAZE (French) 'babbler'. Var., Blaise.

BLISS (Old English) 'bliss'.

BLYTHE (Old English) 'happy'.

BOB see **ROBERT**.

BOLTON (Old English) 'of the farm'. Var., Bolten.

BONIFACE (Latin. Pron: Bonnifass) 'well doer'.

BOOTH (Old German) 'from a market', or 'homelover'.

BORIS (Russian) 'a fighter'.

BOWDEN (Old German) 'bold friend'. Var., Baldwin.

BOWEN (Celtic. Pron: Boen) 'the son or descendant of Owen'.

BOYCE (French) 'dweller in the woodlands'.

BOYD (Celtic) 'light-haired'.

BOYDEN (Celtic) 'herald'.

BRADEN (Old English) 'of the village of sun'.

BRADLEY (Old English) 'from the broad meadow'.

BRAM see **ABRAHAM**.

BRAMWELL (Old English) 'of Bram's well'. Dim., Bram.

BRAND (Scandinavian) 'a flame'.

BRANDON see **BRENDAN**.

BRANT (Old German) 'fiery'.

BRENDAN (Celtic) 'from the fiery hill' or 'stinking hair'. Var., Brandon, Brendon, Brennan.

BRENT (Old English) 'steep hill'.

BRETT (French) 'a native of Brittany'. Var., Bret.

BRIAN (Celtic) 'strong; powerful'. Var., Bryan, Bryant, Brien, Brienns.

BRICE (Celtic) 'swift'. Var., Bryce.

BRIGHAM (Old English) 'dweller by the bridge'.

BRITIUS (Latin) 'man of Brittium'. Var., Brice.

BROCARD (Old German) 'badgers earth'.

BROCK (Celtic) 'badger'.

BROMLEY (Old English) 'a dweller in the meadow'. Var. and dim., Bromlea, Bromleigh, Brom, Lee.

BROOK (English) 'stream'.

BRUCE (French) 'from the brushwood thicket'.

BRUNO (Old German. Pron: Bruno) 'brown'.

BRUTUS (Latin. Pron: Brutus) 'hairy'.

BRYCHAN (Welsh. Pron: Brikan – as in 'loch') 'freckled'.

BRYDEN (Scottish) 'strong'.

BRYN (Welsh. Pron: Brin) 'hill'.

BURGESS (Old German) 'a townsman'. Var. and dim., Bergess, Berger, Berg, Burg.

BURN (Scottish) 'stream'.

BURTON (Old English) 'of bright fame'. Var. and dim., Berton, Bert, Burt.

BYRAM (Old English) 'from the ancient byre'.

C

CADEL (Welsh) 'battle'.

CADIFOR (Welsh) 'stout in battle'.

CADMAR (Celtic) 'brave sailor'. Var., Cadmarr.

CADMON (Celtic) brave warrior'. Var., Cadmann, Cadman,

Caedom (the first Anglo-Saxon poet).

CADVAN (Welsh) 'war horn'.

CADWALLADER (Welsh. Pron: Kadwōllader) 'arranger of battles'.

CAESAR (Latin or Etruscan. Pron: Seeza) 'fleecy head'.

CAILLIN (Welsh 'peace-maker'.

CAIUS (Latin. Pron: Kai-yus) 'rejoiced in'.

CALDER (Celtic. Pron: Kawlder) 'from the river of stones'.

CALEB (Hebrew. Pron: Kayleb) 'bold, impetuous'. Dim., Cal.

CALLUM (Pron: Kalum) Surname used as Christian name in Scotland.

CALVIN (Latin) 'bald'. Var. and dim., Calvert, Cal.

CAMERON (Gaelic) 'crooked nose'. Dim., Cam, Camm.

CAMPBELL (French) 'from a bright field'.

CANTIAN (Latin) name of 4th-century Roman saint martyred under Diocletian.

CARADOC (Welsh–Scottish) 'beloved'.

CAREW (Celtic) 'from this fortress'. Dim., Carr.

CAREY, CARY (Latin) 'dear'.

CARL English rendering of German Karl, see **CHARLES**.

CARLETON (French) probably 'strong man'.

CARLISLE (Latin. Pron:

Karlyl) 'from a walled city; island'. Var., Carlyle.

CARNEY (Celtic) 'valiant soldier'. Var., Carnay.

CAROL variation of Charles.

CARSON (Welsh) 'son of a Carr, Carr's son'.

CARTER (Old English) 'the cart-maker'. Dim., Cart.

CASEY (Irish) 'valorous'.

CASIMIR (Slavonic) 'proclamation of peace'. Var. and dim., Casper, Kazimir, Cass, Cassie, Cassy.

CASPAR, CASS, CASSIE see **CASIMIR, JASPER.**

CASSIAN (Latin) Plant name.

CASSIUS (Latin) The name of one of the eight conspirators against Caesar.

CASTUS (Slavonic) 'honour, glory'.

CATO (Latin) 'cautious'. Var., Caton, Catton.

CAVAN possibly Irish 'comely birth'.

CECIL (Latin. Pron: Sesil) 'blind'.

CEDRIC (Celtic. Pron: Sedrik) 'amiable, friendly', a corruption of Cerdic.

CHAD (Old English) 'war'.

CHADWICK (Celtic) 'the protector'. Old spelling Ceadda.

CHAIM (Origin uncertain, poss. from the Hebrew) 'the Lord will judge'.

CHALMER (Old German) 'king of the household'.

CHANDLER (French) 'candle-maker'. Dim., Chan.

CHANNING (Old English) 'a regent, knowing'.

CHAPMANN (Old English) 'a man of the city, urbane'. Var., Chapman.

CHARLES (Old German) 'man'. Var. and dim., Carey, Carl, Carol, Carrol, Karl, Karol, Charley, Charlie, Chas, Carlo, Carlos, Cary, Chuck.

CHARLTON (Old English) 'of Charles' farm'. Var., Carleton, Carlton, Charleton.

CHENEY (French. Pron: Chayni) 'from the forest of oak trees'. Var., Chenay, Chenee.

CHESTER (Latin) 'of the fortified camp'. Var. and dim., Cheston, Chet.

CHILTON (Old English) 'from the farm by the spring'. Var., Chelton.

CHRISTIAN (Latin) 'a Christian'. Var. and dim., Kristian, Kristin, Chris, Kit.

CHRISTOPHER (Greek) 'Christ-bearer'. Dim., Chris, Christie, Christy, Kit, Kester, Kris, Kriss.

CIBBER (Pron: Sibber) Surname sometimes used as a Christian name, Var., Cybar.

CICERO (Latin) 'chick pea'.

CLARENCE (Old English) possibly 'bright, light'. Dim., Clair, Clare.

CLARK (Latin) 'scholarly, wise'. Var., Clarke.

CLAUD (Latin) 'lame'. Var. and dim., Claude, Claudy.

CLAYTON (Old English) 'mortal man'. Var. and dim., Clayborn, Clayborne, Clay.

CLEMENT (Latin) 'mild; kind; merciful'. Var. and dim., Clemence, Clem.

CLEMOW (Welsh. Pron: Klemo) Dim., of Clement. Var., Clemo.

CLIFFORD (Old English) 'from the ford near the cliff', Dim., Cliff.

CLIFTON (Old English) 'from the farm at the cliff'.

CLINTON (Old English) 'from the headland farm'.

CLIVE (English) 'cliff'. Var., Cleve. Surname of Clive of India, became a Christian name in his honour.

CLOVIS (German–Old French. Pron: Klovis) meaning uncertain – Patron saint of captives.

CLYDE (Celtic) 'heard from a distance'.

COLBY (Old English) 'from the dark farm'. Var. and dim., Colbye, Col, Colb.

COLEMAN (Celtic) 'dove-keeper'. Var. and dim., Colman, Col, Cole.

COLIN (Gaelic) 'gay young dog'. Dim., Cole. See also NICHOLAS.

COLLEY (Old English) 'swarthy – black haired'.

COLTON (Old English) 'of a dark city'. Var., Coltin, Coltun.

COLWYN (Old English) 'a friend from the dark'. Var., Colwen, Colin, Colwin.

CONAL (Irish) 'high-mighty'.

CONAN (Celtic) 'wisdom'. Var., Conran.

CONMAR (Irish) 'great strength'.

CONOR (Irish) 'High desire'.

CONRAD (Old German) 'bold counsel'. Var. and dim., Konrad, Con, Connie, Curt.

CONROY (Irish) 'hound of the plain'.

CONSTANTINE (Latin) 'unwavering; firm'. Var. and dim., Constant, Conn.

CONWAY (Celtic) 'a man of the great plains'.

CORDELL (French) 'binding cord or rope'.

COREY (Celtic. Pron: Kawri) 'ravine dweller'. Var., Cory.

CORIN (Greek) meaning uncertain. Titania mentions him to Oberon in a fit of pique in Act II Scene 1 of *A Midsummer Night's Dream*.

CORNELIUS (Latin) 'battle horn'. Dim., Cornel, Cornell, Neal, Neil.

CORWIN (Old English) 'the raven's friend'. Var., Corwun, Korwin, Korwun.

COSMO (Greek. Pron: Kōzmo) 'universe', or 'in good order', often found in Scotland.

COURTENAY (French. Pron: Kawtni) Place name from the Isle de France. Var. and dim., Courtland, Courtney, Court, Cort, Cortie, Corty.

CRAIG (Celtic) 'of the crag or stony hill'.

CRANOG (Welsh) 'heron'.

CRAWFORD (Old English) 'of the crow's ford'. Var., Crowford.

CRISPIN (Latin) 'curly-haired'. Var., Crispen, Crispian.

CRONON (Old English) possibly variation of Irish 'strong help'.

CROSBY (Old English) 'near the crossroad'.

CULLEN (Celtic) 'pet'.

CULVER (Old English) 'gentle; peaceful; dove'.

CURRAN (origin uncertain) 'heroic; resolute'. Var., Curan.

CURTIS (French) 'courteous'. Dim., Curt, Kurt.

CUTHBERT (Old English) 'famous splendour'. Var., Cuthburt.

CYMBELINE (Celtic. Pron: Simbeleen) 'Lord of the sun'. Dim., Cy.

CYNAN (Welsh) 'chief'.

CYNWELL (Welsh) Probably 'king of power'.

CYRAN (French) 'spear man'. Var., Cyrin.

CYRIL (Greek. Pron: Sirril) 'masterful'.

CYRUS (Persian) 'throne'. Dim', Cy, Rus.

D

DACIAN (Latin. Pron: Daysian) meaning uncertain.

DACRE (French. Pron: Dayker) from the name of a town in Palestine.

DAEGAL (Scandinavian) 'born at daylight'. Var. and dim., Dagall, Dygal, Dygall, Dag.

DAGAN (Scandinavian) 'sunrise'.

DAIG Probably Irish form of the Icelandic Dagr 'day'.

DALE (Old German) 'valley dweller'. Var., Dalton.

DAMON (Greek. Pron: Daymon) 'the tamer'. Var., Damian, Damien.

DANA (Scandinavian) 'a Dane'. Var., Dane.

DANIEL (Hebrew) 'God has judged'. Var. and dim., Daniell, Darnell, Dan, Danny, Deiniol (Welsh form).

DANTE (Pron: Dantay) see DURAND.

DARCY (Pron: Darsi) French place name, also the name of one of the companions of William the Conqueror.

DARIUS (Persian) 'a man of many possessions'. Var., Darian, Derian, Dorian.

DARKON (Hebrew) 'leader; a head of the tribe'. Var., Darkkon, Derkon, Dorkan.

DARRYL (Old English. Pron: Darril) 'beloved'. Var., Darrel, Darrol.

DARSHAN (Indian) probably 'gift of God'.

DAVE see **DAVID**.

DAVID (Hebrew) 'beloved'. Var. and dim., Dave, Davie, Davis, Davy.

DEAN (Old English) 'valley'.

DECLAN (Pron: Deklan) the name of a 6th-century Irish saint.

DEMETRIAN (Greek. Pron: Demeetrian) see **DEMETRIUS**.

DEMETRIUS (Greek) 'lover of the earth'. Var. and dim., Dimitri, Dmitri.

DEMPSTER (Old English. Pron: Demster) 'a judge; wise'. Var. and dim., Dempstor, Dempsey.

DENBY (Scandinavian) 'from the Danish settlement; a loyal Dane'. Var., Danby.

DENHOLM (English. Pron: Dennem) 'home of Dionysius'. Var., Denholme.

DENNIS (Greek) 'of Dionysius'. Var. and dim., Denis, Dennison, Denys, Denzil, Dion, Dennie, Denny, Deny.

DENZELL Cornish place name. Var., Denzil, Danzil.

DEREK, DERRICK, DERK

A diminutive of the Old German Theodoric 'folk ruler'.

DERMOT see **DIARMID**.

DERREN (Irish) 'uncertain'. Var. and dim., Deryn, Derry.

DERWIN (Old German) 'animal lover'. Var. and dim., Derwon, Dorwin, Durwin, Derr, Dorr, Durr, Win.

DESMOND (Celtic) 'worldly; sophisticated'. Dim., Desi.

DEVIN (Celtic) 'a poet'.

DEXTER (Latin) 'right-handed: dexterous'.

DIARMID (Old Irish. Pron: Diermid) 'free from envy'. Var., Diarmid, Diarmit, Diarmis.

DIBRI (Hebrew) 'eloquent and forthright'. Var., Dibrin, Dibbrun, Dibru.

DICK see **RICHARD**.

DICKON Mediaeval dim. of **RICHARD**.

DIGBY (Old English) 'from the settlement by the dyke'.

DILLION (Celtic) 'faithful'. Var., Dilion.

DILLWYN (Welsh) Probably from the Latin 'God's worshipper'.

DINSDALE (Welsh) 'born on Sunday'.

DION (Pron: Dyon) see **DENNIS**.

DIXON (German) 'blessed'.

DOEL (English) possibly 'sorrows'.

DOMINIC (Latin) 'the

Lord's'. Var. and dim., Dominick, Dom, Domenick, Dominey, Nic, Nick, Nicky.

DONAL see **DONALD.**

DONALBAIN (Scottish) 'proud chief' – Shakespeare may have added the last part.

DONALD (Celtic) 'ruler of the world'. Var. and dim., Donal, Donall, Donnell, Don, Donn, Donnie, Donny.

DONAT (Latin) 'given'. Var. and dim., Donatus.

DORAN (Greek) 'the stranger'. Var., Dorran.

DORIAN (Latin–Greek) 'from Doris in Ancient Greece'. Dim., Dore, Dorey, Dory.

DOUGAL (Celtic) 'dark stranger'. Var., Dugald.

DOUGLAS (Celtic) 'from the dark blue stream'.

DOYLE (Celtic) 'the dark stranger; newcomer'.

DOYNE (English) meaning uncertain.

DREW (Old German) 'skilled; honest'. Var., Dru, Drue.

DRISCOLL (Celtic) 'the speaker or interpreter'.

DRUCE (Celtic) 'wise man; capable and adept'.

DUDLEY (Old English) 'a place'. Dim., Dud, Lee.

DUER (Celtic. Pron: Dyuer) 'valorous in battle'. Var., Dur.

DUKE (Latin) 'leader'.

DUNCAN (Celtic) 'brown warrior'. Dim., Dunc.

DUNSTAN (Old English) 'hill stone'.

DURAND (Latin. Pron: Dyurand) 'enduring'. Var., Dante, Durant.

DURWARD (Old English) 'the doorkeeper'. Var., Durware, Durwood, Derwood.

DURWIN (Old English) 'dear friend'. Var., Durwyn.

DUSTIN (Old German) 'strong hearted leader'. Var., Dustin, Durston, Durst.

DWAYNE (Gaelic) 'poem; song'. Var., Duan, Duane

DYSART English family name taken from place name.

E

EAMON Irish form of Edmond.

EARL (Old English) 'nobleman; chief'. Var., Earle, Early, Erle, Errol, Airell.

EARNEST (Old English) 'Eagle stone'.

EDAN (Celtic) 'flame'. Var., Eden.

EDBERT (Old English) 'a generous soul'. Var., Eadbertas, Eadbertus.

EDEN (Hebrew) 'delight'.

EDGAR (Old English) 'lucky spear; fortunate warrior'. Dim., Ed, Eddie, Eddy.

EDLAN (Old English) 'from the prosperous village'.

EDMUND (Old English) 'richly protected'. Var. and dim., Edmond, Ed, Eddie, Ned, Neddy, Eamon.

EDREI (Hebrew) 'powerful leader'. Var., Edroi.

EDRIC (Old English) 'rich ruler'. Var. and dim., Edrick, Edrock, Dric.

EDSEL (Old English) 'profound; deep thinker'.

EDSON (Old English) 'the son of Ed'. Var., Edison.

EDWARD (Old English) 'happily protected'. Var. and dim., Eduard, Ed, Eddie, Ned, Neddy, Ted, Teddy.

EDWIN (Old English) 'happy friend'. Var. and dim., Edlin, Ed, Eddie, Eddy, Edwin.

EILAN (Irish) 'light'.

EIRAN (Irish) 'peace'.

ELDON (Old German) 'respected; older'. Var. and dim., Elden, Eldon, El.

ELDRIDGE (Old English) 'wise advisor'. Var., Eldred.

ELDWIN (Old English) 'so wise; advisor'. Var., Eldwen, Eldwon, Eldwun.

ELEAZAR (Hebrew. Pron: Eleeayzer) 'helped by God'. Var., Eliezer, Lazarus, Lazar.

ELGAR (Old English) 'noble spear'. Also the surname of the famous English composer.

ELI (Hebrew) 'the highest'. Var., Elia, Ely.

ELIAN (Latin) 'bright'.

ELIAS (Hebrew. Pron: Elias) 'the Lord is God'. Var., Elihu, Elijah, Eliot, Elliott, Ellis.

ELIGIUS (Latin) 'a metal worker'. Var., Eligias, Eligium, Eloi, Elloi.

ELLARD (Old German) 'nobly brave; warrior'. Var., Ellerd, Ellord, Elurd.

ELLERY (Old German) 'of the elder trees'. Var., Elery.

ELLIOT see **ELIAS**.

ELLIS Anglicized version of Elijah and Elisha.

ELON (Hebrew) 'mighty oak; invincible'. Var., Elon, Elun.

ELROY (Latin) 'royal'. Var. and dim., Leroy, Roy.

ELSTAN (Old English) 'the little one; small stone'. Var., Elston, Elfstan.

ELTON (Old English) 'from the old farm or village'.

ELVIN see **ALVIN**.

EMERICK (Old German) 'ruler'. Var. and dim., Emmerich, Emery.

EMIL (German–Latin) 'striver'.

EMLYN (Welsh. Pron: Emlin) came perhaps from the Latin name Aemilianus 'earnestness'.

EMMANUEL (Hebrew) 'God is with us'. Var. and dim., Imannuel, Mannel, Manny.

EMMET (Old English) 'Ant; industrious'.

ENDYMION (Greek. Pron: Endimion) The shepherd who

was loved by Artemis, Apollo's chaste sister.

EPHRAIM (Hebrew) 'meadows'.

ERASMUS (Greek. Pron: Erazmus) 'beloved'.

ERIC (Old German) 'ruler'. Norse Eirik. Var., Erich.

ERNAN Irish version of **EARNEST**.

ERROL see **EARL**.

ERSKINE (Celtic) of uncertain meaning.

ERWIN Var., Eurwen.

ERYK (Polish) 'Ever king'.

ESAU (Hebrew. Pron: Eesaw) 'noted for his hair; long hair'.

ESKILL (Scandinavian) 'a protestor'. Var., Eskil.

ESMOND (Old English) 'gracious protector'.

EUGENE (Greek. Pron: Yujeen) 'noble; well born'. Dim., Gene.

EUSTACE (Greek. Pron: Yustas) 'fruitful'. Var. dim., Eustas.

EVAN Welsh form of John.

EVANDER (Greek) 'benefactor'. Dim., Evan.

EVELYN (Old English. Pron: Evlin) 'a dear youth'. Var. and dim., Avelin, Evelinn, Evelunn, Evel, Lynn.

EVENTIUS (Latin) 'long-awaited'. Var., Eventias, Eventos, Eventus.

EVERARD (Old German)

'mighty as a boar'. Var. and dim., Eberhart, Everett, Ev.

EWALD (Latin: Pron: Yuald) 'the bearer of good news'. Var. and dim., Ewold, Wald.

EWART (English) 'strong wild boar'.

EWEN (Scottish. Pron: Yuen) 'high born youth'. Var. and dim., Ewan, Ewin.

EYMON (Welsh) 'Anvil-stability'.

EZEKIEL (Hebrew) 'may God strenghen'. Dim., Zeke.

EZRA (Hebrew) 'the helpful or helper'. Dim., Ez.

F

FABIAN (Latin. Pron: Faybian) 'grower of beans'. Dim., Fabe, Fabyan.

FAIRFAX (Old English) 'fair or yellow-haired'.

FAIRLEY (Old English) 'from the far meadow'. Var. and dim., Fairlie, Farley, Farl.

FALKNER (Old English. Pron: Fawkner) 'falcon hunter or trainer'. Var., Faulkner, Fowler.

FARLEY see **FAIRLEY**.

FARMANN (Old English) 'a sojourner'. Var., Farman, Farmound, Farmun.

FARQUHAR (Gothic. Pron: Farkar) 'friendly man'.

FARRELL (Celtic) 'the valorous one'. Var., Farrel.

FARREN (Anglicized version of Ferdinand.

FAUSTUS (Latin) 'strong opponent'. Dim., Faust.

FAVIAN (Latin) 'a man of understanding'. Var., Favianus, Favien, Fabin.

FEARNLEY (Old English) Found often in Cornwall, probably 'fern meadow'. Var., Fearnleigh, Fernley, Feanley.

FEDELM (Irish-German) 'helmet'.

FEIOLIM (Irish) 'the ever good'.

FELIX (Latin) 'happy'.

FENTON (Old English) 'dweller of the marshland'.

FERDINAND (Old German) 'bold venture'. Var. and dim., Ferde, Fernand, Fernando, Hernando, Ferd, Ferdie.

FERDY dim., of Ferdinand now a name in its own right.

FERGUS (Celtic) 'chosen one'. Var., Fargus.

FERRAN Catalan dim. of Ferdinand.

FERRIS (Celtic) 'rock'.

FIACHAN (Irish–German) 'wisdom'.

FIDEL (Latin. Pron: Feedel) 'faithful; true'. Var., Fidelis.

FILLAN The name of a 9th-century Irish saint who went to Scotland. The place where he died is now called Strathfillan. Var., Foelan.

FINBAR (Irish) 'white haired'. Var., Finbur.

FINIAN (Irish) 'fair children'.

FINLAY (Gaelic) 'fair hero'.

FINTAN (Irish) 'white'.

FIRMIN meaning uncertain. There was a 6th-century saint called St. Firminus.

FISK (Scandinavian) 'the fisherman'. Var., Fiske.

FITZGERALD (Old German) 'a son of Gerald'. Dim., Fitz, Fitzger, Gerry.

FITZPATRICK (Old German) 'a son of Patrick'. Dim., Fitz, Fitzpat, Patrick.

FLAVIAN (Latin. Pron: Flayvian) 'flaxen haired'. Var., Flavius.

FLEMING (Old English) 'the Dutchman'. Dim., Flem.

FLORIAN (Latin) 'flourishing'. Dim., Flory. The name of the 4th-century Roman saint invoked against fire and drought.

FLOYD see LLOYD.

FORGAEL (Irish 'man of strength'. Var., Ferghal.

FORREST (Old German) 'from the woods'. Var., Forest.

FOSTER (Old German) 'forester; keeper of the preserve'.

FRANCIS (Latin) 'a Frenchman'. St. Francis of Assisi made the name popular. Var. and dim., Frank, Franchot, Franz, Frankie, Fran.

FRANK (Old German) Franco 'A frank'. Var. and dim., Francis, Franco.

FRANKLIN (Old German) 'a free man'. Dim., Frank.

FREDERICK (Old German) 'peaceful chieftain'. Var. and dim., Frederic, Fredric, Fred, Freddie, Freddy, Fritz, Frederigo.

FREEMAN (Old English) 'one born free'. Var., Freemon.

FRITH (Old English) 'peace'.

FRITZ see FREDERICK.

FULKE (Old German) 'the people'. Var. and dim., Fawke, Fulcher, Fulco.

FULTON (Old English) 'from a field or farm town'. Surname used as Christian name in Scotland.

G

GABOR (Hungarian) 'hero of God'.

GABRIEL (Hebrew) 'strongman of God'. Dim., Gabby, Gabe. Var., Gabryell.

GALAHAD (Welsh) The name of the knight who found the Holy Grail.

GALLEN (Greek) 'healer'.

GALLIN probably Celtic 'little stranger'.

GALVIN (Celtic) 'the sparrow'. Dim., Vin, Vinny.

GAMALIEL (Hebrew. Pron: Gamayliel) 'God is my recompense'.

GAMEL (Old Norse) 'ancient'.

GARDELL (Old German) 'wary guard; careful'. Var., Gardal, Gardel, Gardol.

GARDINER (Old German) 'flower lover'. Var., Gardner.

GARETH (Welsh) meaning obscure. Appears in Tennyson's poem 'Gareth and Lynnet'.

GARFIELD (English), 'spearfield', found often in Cornwall.

GARNER (Old German) 'the defender; noble guardian'.

GARNET (Anglo-Norman) 'grain; red jewel'. Var., Garnett.

GARRET (Old German) 'to preserve'. Var. and dim., Gareth, Garrett, Garett, Garth, Gerard, Garry, Gary, Gerry, Jaret, Jary.

GARRICK (Old English) 'spear rule'. Dim., Rick.

GARTH (Scandinavian) 'enclosure'.

GARVIN (Old German) 'battle friend'. Dim., Gar, Gary.

GARY see GARRETT, GARVIN.

GASPER see JASPER.

GASTON (Old French) 'from Gascony'. Var., Gascon.

GATHHEM (Hebrew) 'winelover'. Var., Gathe.

GATIAN (Hebrew) 'from a venerated family'. Var. and dim., Gatias, Gati.

GAVIN (Old German) 'white hawk or battle hawk'.

GAYLORD (French) 'merry, happy' from 'Galliard'.

GAYNOR a variation of **GAYLORD**.

GAWAIN the old way of spelling **GAVIN**.

GAZO (Hebrew) 'a powerful leader'. Var., Gazzo.

GENE (Pron: Jeen) see **EUGENE**.

GEOFFREY (Old German) 'traveller in a peaceful land'. Var. and dim., Jeffers, Jeffrey, Jeffry, Geof, Geoff, Jeff.

GEORGE (Greek) 'tiller of the soil'. Var. and dim., Georges, Jorge, Jorin, Joris, Jurgen, Georgie.

GERAINT (Welsh form of old British **GERONTIUS**. Pron: Geraynt) 'ancient'.

GERALD (Old German) 'mighty spearman'. Var. and dim., Garold, Gereld, Gerrald, Jereld, Jerold, Jerrold, Gerry, Gery, Jer, Jerry.

GERARD (Old German) 'spear hard'.

GERLAND (Old English) 'crowned in great honour'. Var., Garland, Garlan.

GERMINIAN (Latin: Pron: Jeminnian) 'born in May'. Var., Geminius.

GERRY see **GARRETT**, **GERALD**.

GERSHOM (Hebrew) 'bell' Var., Gersho, Gershom, Gorsham, Gorsh.

GERVASE (Old German.

Pron: Jervays) 'servant of the spear' or 'honourable'. Var. and dim., Gervais, Jarvis, Jervis, Jarv, Jarvey.

GIBEON (Hebrew) 'born on the hill'. Var. and dim., Gibbeon, Gibbon, Gibun, Gibe, Gibby, Gibbie.

GIBRIAN (Latin) 'from a high place; aristocrat; stern'. Var., Gibryon.

GIDEON (Hebrew) 'one handed; stumpy'.

GIFFARD (Old German) 'fierce gift'.

GILBERT (Old German) 'bright pledge'. Var. and dim., Gilpin, Wilbert, Wilbur, Gil.

GILCHRIST (Gaelic) 'servant of Christ'. Var., Gilly.

GILDAS (Latin) 'of wise heritage'. Var. and dim., Gildus, Gilus, Gil.

GILEAD (Hebrew) 'of a rocky region'. Var., Gillead, Gilleod, Gilud.

GILES (Greek) 'kid'. Var. and dim., Gilles, Gil.

GILMOUR (Old English) 'servant of Mary'.

GILROY (Latin) 'the king's faithful servant'.

GIRVAN (Probably Hebrew) 'the Lord's Grace'.

GLAYS (Welsh) 'lame'.

GLEN (Celtic) 'from the valley'. Var., Glenn, Glynn.

GLYNDWR (Welsh) 'from the valley'.

GODDARD (Old German) 'God, hard; of a firm nature'. Var., Godderd, Goddord, Godred.

GODFREY (Old German) 'God's peace'.

GODRIC (Old English) 'God-ruler'.

GOODMAN (Old German) 'good man'. Dim., Goody.

GOODWIN (Old German) 'good and faithful friend'. Var., Gladwin, Godwin.

GORAN meaning uncertain. The name of a 6th-century Cornish saint who was a friend of St. Patrick.

GORDON Scottish place name made popular as a Christian name by Gealner Gordon.

GORE maybe from the Norwegian 'war serpent'.

GOWER probably from the Dutch 'God's peace'.

GRAEME Gaelic spelling of **GRAHAM**.

GRAHAM (Pron: Grayem) Scottish place name commandeered for use as Christian name by an illustrious Scottish family.

GRANT (French) 'great'.

GRANVILLE (French) 'of the big town'. Var., Grenville, originally a surname derived from Granville in Normandy.

GRAYSON (Old English) 'a judge's son'. Var. and dim., Greyson, Greysun, Greyso, Gray, Grey.

GREGORY (Greek) 'vigilant'. Dim., Greg.

GRESHAM (Old English) 'from the grazing land',

GRIFFITH (Welsh) 'red-haired'. Var. and dim., Griffin, Rufus, Griff, Rufe.

GUNTHER (Old German) 'bold warrior'. Var., Gunar, Guntar, Gunter, Gunthar.

GURIAS (Hebrew) 'from a wandering family'. Var., Guriastus, Guriustus.

GUS see **AUGUSTUS**.

GUSTAVE (Scandinavian) possibly 'to meditate' or 'staff'. Var. and dim., Gustaf, Gustavus, Gus, Gussie.

GUTHRIE (Celtic) 'war serpent', or 'war hero'.

GUY (Old German) 'wood or wide'. Var., Guido, Guyon, Wiatt, Wyatt.

GWENFIL (Welsh) 'white'.

GWILLIAM (Irish form of William).

GWYN (Celtic) 'fair'. Var., Guin, Gynn.

H

HACON (Scandinavian) 'high race'.

HADRIAN (Latin) 'of the Adriatic'.

HADWIN (Old German) 'dear friend in battle'. Var. and dim., Hadwyn, Wynn.

HAEMON (Old German. Pron: Haymon) 'home'. Var., Hayman, Hamon.

HAGAR probably Hebrew 'festival'.

HAINES (Old German) 'from a vined cottage'. Var., Hannus, Hanus, Haynes.

HAL see HAROLD, HENRY.

HALAND (Old English) 'of Henry's land'. Var. and dim., Halland, Hall, Hal.

HALDEN (Old German) 'half Dane'. Var., Haldane.

HALSEY (Old English) 'from Hal's island'. Var., Halsy.

HAMILTON (French) 'from the mountain hamlet'.

HAMISH see JAMES.

HAMON (Old German) 'home'. Var. and dim., Hamelen, Hamo.

HANFORD (Old German) 'from the tall ford'. Var., Hanforrd, Hanfurd.

HANLEY (Old English) 'of the high meadow'. Var. and dim., Hanleigh, Henleigh, Henley, Henry.

HANNIBAL (Phoenician) The name of the great Carthaginian general.

HANS see JOHN.

HANSEL (Scandinavian) 'a gift from the Lord'.

HARCOURT (French) 'from an armed court'.

HARDY (Old German) 'from a hardy stock'. Var. and dim., Harday, Hardi, Ard.

HARLAN (Old German) 'from the battle land'.

HARLEY (Old English) from the deer's meadow'. Var. and dim., Harden, Harleigh, Hartley, Arley, Arlie, Harl, Hart.

HAROLD (Old English) 'army commander'. Var. and dim., Harald, Herald, Hereld, Herold, Herrick, Hal, Harry, Harrold.

HARRIS (Old English) 'a son of Henry'. Var. and dim., Harrus, Harri.

HARRY see HAROLD, HENRY.

HARTLEY (English) originally a surname taken from the place name.

HARTON (English) 'fortified city'.

HARTWELL (Old German) 'from the deer's spring'. Var. and dim., Harwell, Harwill, Hart.

HARVEY (Old Breton) 'bitter'. Var. and dim., Hervey, Harv, Harve, Herv, Herve.

HAYDEN (Old German) 'from the hedged hill'. Var., Haydn.

HAYES (Old English) 'from the woods; the hunter'.

HEATH (English) 'heathland'.

HECTOR (Greek) 'steadfast'. Dim., Heck. The name of Priam's heroic son.

HEDGER (English) probably 'war refuge'.

HEDLEY surname often used

as a Christian name in Cornwall.

HENLEY see HANLEY.

HENRY (Old German) 'ruler of the house'. Var. and dim., Enrico, Hamlin, Heinrick, Hendrick, Hendrik, Henri, Hal, Hank, Harry, Hen, Henry.

HERBERT (Old German) 'bright warrior'. Dim., Bert, Bertie, Herb, Herbie.

HEREWARD (Old English) Hereward the Wake was the last leader of the Saxons against the Normans.

HERMAN (Old German) 'noble warrior'. Var. and dim., Armand, Armin, Armond, Armyn, Hermon, Herm, Hermie.

HERON (English) probably 'holy name'. Var., Hieron.

HERWIN (Old German) 'a friend or lover of battle'.

HEYWOOD (Old German) 'from the dark green forest'.

HIAM (Hebrew) probably 'the Lord will judge'.

HILARY (Latin) 'cheerful; merry'. Var., Hilaire, Hillary.

HILLIARD (Old German) 'war guardian or protector'.

HILTON (Old English) 'from the house on the hill'. Var., Hiltan, Hilten.

HIRAM (Hebrew) 'God is exalted'. Dim., Hy.

HOBART see HUBERT.

HOLBROOK (Old English) 'from the valley brook'.

HOLDEN (Old German) 'kind'.

HOLLIS (Old English) 'dweller by the holly trees'.

HOLMANN (Old German) 'from the river island'. Var., Holman, Holmen, Holmun.

HOLMES (Old German) 'son of Holmann'. Var., Holms.

HOMER (Greek) 'pledge'.

HORACE (Latin) meaning uncertain. The most famous bearer of the name is the Roman poet Horace.

HORATIO (Pron: Horayshio) see HORACE.

HOSEA (Hebrew. Pron: Hozeea) 'salvation'. Var., Hosia.

HOUSTON (Old English) 'from a mountain town'.

HOWARD (Old German) 'heart; soul protection'. Dim., Howie.

HOWLAND (Old English) 'of the hills'. Var., Howlend, Howlond, Howlyn.

HUBERT (Old German) 'shining of mind'. Var. and dim., Hobart, Hoyt, Hubbard, Hubie.

HUGH (Old German) 'heart'. Var. and dim., Hugo, Huey, Hughes, Hugo, Hughie, Huelin.

HUGO see HUGH.

HUMBERT (Old German) 'bright home'. Dim., Bert, Bertie.

HUME (Old German) 'lover of his home'. Var., Humo.

HUMPHREY (Old English) 'giant, peace; a protector of peace'. Var. and dim., Humfrey.

HUNTER (Old English) 'the hunter'. Var., Huntley.

HYMAN (Hebrew) 'life', masculine of Eve. Var. and dim., Hymon, Hy, Hymie.

HYWEL (Welsh) 'eminent'. Var. and dim., Hoel, Hough.

I

IAN – Iain – Scottish version of JOHN.

IDRIS (Welsh) 'fiery lord'.

IGNATIUS (Latin) 'the fiery and the ardent'. Var. and dim., Ignace, Ignatz.

IGOR (Russian. Pron: Eegaw) name originating in Scandinavia, 'hero', Var., Igne, Ingmar.

IMMANUEL see **EMMANUEL.**

INAN Irish form of Evan.

INGRAM (Old German) 'angel; hero; raven'. Var., Ingraham.

INIGO (Greek) meaning uncertain. The name spread due to St. Ignatius de Loyola, founder of the Jesuits.

INNES (Celtic. Pron: Inniss) 'from the island'. Var., Innis.

IOLO (Welsh) 'worthy lord'. Nick-name derived from the old Welsh name Iorwerth.

IRVIN (Old English) 'sea friend'. Var. and dim., Ervin, Ervine, Erwin, Irving, Irwin, Marvin, Mervin, Merwin.

IRVING see **IRVIN.**

IRWIN see **IRVIN.**

ISAAC (Hebrew) 'God smiles on him'. Var. and dim., Isac, Izaak, Izzy.

ISHMAEL (Hebrew) 'the wanderer'. Var. and dim., Ishmul, Ishy, Ish.

ISIDORE (Greek) 'a gift'. Var. and dim., Isador, Isadore, Isidor, Dore, Dorian, Dory, Issy, Iz, Izzy.

ISLWYN (Welsh) 'friend'.

ISMAN (Hebrew) 'a loyal husband'. Var., Isma.

ISRAEL (Hebrew) 'the Lord's warrior or soldier'. Dim., Issy, Iz, Izzy.

ITHNAN (Hebrew) 'the strong sailor'.

IVAN see **JOHN.**

IVAR (Scandinavian) 'military archer'. Var., Iver, Ives, Ivon, Ivor, Ivo, Yves, Ifor, Irah.

IVES (Pron: Eev) see **IVAR, YVES.**

IVO (Old French) 'yew tree'. Var., Yvon, Yves.

J

JACK see **JOHN.**

JACOB see **JAMES.**

JADDAH (Hebrew) 'a man of wisdom'. Var., Jaddan, Jaddon, Jaddo.

JAGO a name invented by John Galsworthy the novelist who wrote *The Forsyte Saga.*

JAIR (Hebrew) 'a man whom God has enlightened'.

JAKE (Hebrew) 'pious'. Dim., Jacob.

JAMES (Hebrew) 'taken by the heel'. Var. and dim., Hamish, Jacob, Jacques, Seamus, Shamus, Jack, Jake, Jakie, Jamesy, Jamie, Jem, Jemmie, Jemmy, Jim, Jimmie, Jimmy, Jock, Jocko.

JAMESON (English) 'son of James'.

JAMIN (Hebrew) 'right-handed'. Var., Jammin.

JANAN (Hebrew) 'grace of the Lord'.

JANUARIUS (Latin) 'Born in January'. Var. and dim., Januarias, Janis, Janus.

JAPHETH (Hebrew) 'who grows greater'. Var., Japeth.

JAREBB (Hebrew) 'lively son'. Var., Jareb.

JARED (Hebrew–Arabic) 'the rose'.

JARLATH (Latin) 'a man of control'. Var. and dim., Jarlathus, Jarl.

JARON probably anglicized version of Bohemian 'firm peace'.

JARVIS see **GERVASE.**

JASON (Greek) 'the healer'.

JASPER (Origin uncertain) 'treasure-bringer'. Var. and dim., Caspar, Gaspar, Kaspar, Cass.

JAY (Old English) 'crow' or 'lively'. Also used as a dim. for names beginning with the initial J.

JEFFREY see **GEOFFREY.**

JEGAR (Hebrew) 'witness our love'. Var., Jeggar, Jegger, Jeguar, Jegur.

JEHIAH (Hebrew) 'his life is Jehovah's'. Var., Jehias, Jehius, Johiah.

JEHIEL (Hebrew) 'the son of Jehovah'. Var., Jehial, Jehiell, Jehiul.

JEPHUM (Hebrew) 'he is prepared'. Var., Jepum.

JEREMIAH see **JEREMY.**

JEREMY (Hebrew) 'exalted by God'. Var. and dim., Jeremiah, Jeremias, Jerry.

JERMYN (Latin) 'a German'. Var. and dim., Germaine, Jermalne, Gerry, Jer, Jerry.

JEROME (Greek. Pron: Jerōm) 'sacred name'. Dim., Jer, Jerry.

JERROLD, JERELD, JEROLD see **GERALD .**

JERVIS (Pron: Jarvis), see **GERVASE.**

JESHER (Hebrew) 'an upright man'. Dim., Jesh.

JESSE (Hebrew) 'God lives'. Var. and dim., Jessee, Jess, Jessie.

JESTYN (Latin) 'the just'.

JETHRO (Hebrew) 'abundance; excellence'. Dim., Jeth.

JEVON Welsh form of John, 'favoured of God'.

JIM see JAMES.

JOAB (Hebrew) 'God is his father'. Var., Joub.

JOACHIM (Hebrew) 'may God raise him up'.

JOASH (Hebrew) 'loved by God'. Var., Joashus, Joashis, Joshas, Joshus.

JOB (Hebrew) 'the persecuted; the afflicted'.

JOCK see JAMES, JOHN.

JOEL (Hebrew) 'Jehovah is God'. Dim., Joe, Joey.

JOHANAN (Hebrew) original of JOHN.

JOHN (Hebrew) 'favoured of God'. Var. and dim., Evan, Gian, Giovanni, Hans, Ian, Ivan, Jan, Jevon, Johan, Johann, Jon, Juan, Sean, Shane, Shawn, Zane, Jack, Jock, Johnnie, Johnny, Jonnie, Jonny.

JOHNSTON (Scotch) 'the son of John'. Var., Johnsten, Johnsenn.

JOKTAN (Hebrew) 'tiny one'. Var., Jokkton.

JOLYON (Pron: Jolīon), see JULIAN.

JONAH (Hebrew) 'dove'.

JONAS (Hebrew) 'dove'. Var., Jonah, Jone.

JONATHAN (Hebrew) 'gift of the Lord'. Dim., Jon.

JORDAN (Hebrew) 'flowing down'.

JOSEPH (Hebrew) 'God shall add to him'. Var. and dim., José, Joe, Joey, Jos.

JOSHUA (Hebrew) 'whom God helps'. Dim., Josh.

JOSIAH (Hebrew) 'may God heal' (i.e. the mother at birth). Var., Joseha, Jusha, Joshia.

JOSS, dim. of Josiah now a name in its own right.

JOTHAM (Hebrew) 'God is perfect'. Dim., Joe.

JUDD (Hebrew) 'beloved descendant'. Var. and dim., Jadd, Jedd, Judus, Jud.

JUDSON (Old German) 'the son of Judd'. Var., Jedson, Judsen, Juduson.

JULES see JULIUS.

JULIAN Latin derivative of Julius.

JULIUS (Latin) The Romans thought it was taken from a Greek word 'downy'. Var. and dim., Joliet, Jules, Julian, Jule, Juley, Julie.

JUSTIN (Latin) 'the just'. Var. and dim., Justus, Just.

JUSTINIAN (Latin) a derivative of Justinus. See JUSTIN.

JUVENAL (Latin) 'a man who is venerated; a soothsayer'. Var., Juvenalis, Juventinus.

K

KANE (Celtic) 'bright; radiant'. Var., Kayne.

KARL see **CHARLES.**

KARSTEN (Greek) 'blessed one'. Var. and dim., Kersten, Kirsten, Kirt.

KASPAR see **JASPER.**

KEAN (Irish) 'vast'.

KEEGAN (Celtic) 'high spirited'. Var., Mackeegan, Magan, Megan.

KEIDRYCH (Welsh) possibly from the Breton 'beloved'.

KEITH (Celtic) Scottish surname derived from a place name.

KELBY (Old German) 'from a farm'. Var., Kilby.

KELSEY (Old German) 'from the water'. Var., Kelcey.

KELWIN (Celtic) 'dweller by the water'. Var. and dim., Kelwen, Kelwunn, Kelley,

KENAZ (Hebrew) 'hunter'.

KENDALL (Celtic) 'chief of the valley'. Var. and dim., Kendal, Ken, Kenny.

KENDRICK (Old English) 'royal ruler'. Var. and dim., Kendricks, Kenric, Ken.

KENELM (Old English) 'brave helmet'. Dim., Ken.

KENLEY (Old English) 'of the King's meadow'. Var., Kenlay, Kenlee, Kenleigh.

KENNETH (Gaelic) 'comely'. Var. and dim., Kennet, Ken, Kenny, Kent. The name of the first King of Scotland.

KENRICK (Old English) 'royal ruler'. Var., Kendrick.

KENT see **KENNETH.**

KENTIGERN (Gaelic) The patron saint of Glasgow, 'chief lord'.

KENSYN may be a variation of the Scots 'comely'.

KENWAY (Old English) 'the brave soldier'. Var., Kenwee, Kenweigh, Kenay.

KENYON (Celtic) 'fair-haired'. Dim., Ken, Kenny.

KERBY see **KIRBY.**

KERMIT (Celtic) 'free'. Var. and dim., Dermot, Kerry.

KERRIN (Celtic) 'dark; mysterious'. Var. and dim., Kerr, Kerrie, Kerry.

KERWIN (Celtic) 'dark'. Var., Kerwon, Corwin.

KESTER see **CHRISTOPHER.**

KEVIN (Irish) 'comely birth'. Dim., Kev, Kevan.

KIERON (Celtic) 'dark'. Var., Kieran, Kyran.

KILIAN (Celtic) 'most innocent'. Var., Kilan.

KIMBALL (Old English) 'royally brave'. Var. and dim., Kemble, Kimble, Kim.

KINGSLEY (Old English) 'from the king's meadow'.

KIRBY (Old German) 'from the church village'. Var. and dim., Kerby, Kerr.

KIRIT (Irish) probably 'spearman'.

KIRK (Scandinavian) 'of the church; living close to the church'. Var., Kerk.

KIT see **CHRISTOPHER**.

KONRAD see **CONRAD**.

KURT see **CURTIS**.

KYLE (Gaelic) 'fair and handsome'. Var., Kile.

KYNAN see **CONAL**.

KYNASTON (Welsh) 'chief'.

L

LACHLAN (Celtic) 'warlike'.

LAIRD (Celtic) 'proprietor'.

LAMBERT (Old German) 'bright land'. Dim., Bert, Lam.

LAMONT (Scandinavian) 'a lawyer'. Var., Lamond.

LANDERS (Old English) 'of the land'. Var., Landis, Landure, Landurs.

LANDIS (Old German) 'native'.

LANDON (Old English) 'from the long hill'. Var., Langdon, Langston, Langley.

LANDRY (Old English) 'the local ruler'. Var. and dim., Landre, Landri, Lan.

LANE (Old English) 'lane'.

LANG (Old German) 'tall'.

LANGDON see **LANDON**.

LARS see **LAWRENCE**.

LATHAAM (Old German. Pron: Laytham) 'lives nearby'. Var., Latham.

LATIMER (Old English) 'Latin master or teacher'.

LAUNCELOT (Pron: Lancelot) French diminutive of Old German Lance, 'land'. Var. and dim., Lancelot, Launce, Lance, Lancey.

LAWRENCE (Latin) 'laurel; crowned with laurel'. Var. and dim., Lauren, Laurence, Laurent, Loren, Lorenz, Lorenzo, Lorin, Larry, Lars, Laurie, Lori, Lorry.

LEANDER (Greek. Pron: Leeander) 'lion-man'. Var., Leigh.

LEIGH (Old English) variation of **LELAND**.

LELAND (Old English) 'of the meadowlands'. Var., Leeland, Leigh, Leighland, Leyland.

LEMUEL (Hebrew) 'devoted to God'.

LENOX (Gaelic) 'chief'. Var., Lennox.

LEO (Latin) 'lion'. Var. and dim., Leon, Lion, Lionel, Lyon, Len, Lennie, Lenny.

LEOFRIC (Old English) 'dear ruler'.

LEONIDE (French) 'strong as a lion'.

LEONARD (Old German) 'brave lion'.

LEOPOLD (Old German) 'brave people'. Dim., Leo, Lepp.

LEROY see ELROY.

LESLIE A well known Scottish surname used as a Christian name in England for the last 70 years. Var. and dim., Lesley (usually fem.), Les.

LESTER (Old English) 'from the army or camp'. Var. and dim., Leicester, Les.

LEVI (Hebrew) 'he is one; joined'. Var., Levy.

LEWIS (Old German) 're-nowned in battle'. Var. and dim., Clovis, Lewes, Louis, Ludovick, Lew, Lou, Louie.

LEYLAND see LELAND.

LIAM Irish for William.

LINCOLN (Celtic) 'from the place by the pool; river bank'. Dim., Linc.

LINDLEY (Old English) 'of the Linden tree'. Var., Lindly, Lindsay, Lyndon, Lindsey, Lindy, Lyndon.

LINUS (Hebrew) 'flaxen-haired'. Var., Linis.

LIONEL see LEO.

LIVINGSTON (Old English) 'from a beloved place'.

LLEWELLYN (Celtic) 'lion or leader'. Var., Llywelyn.

LLOYD (Celtic) 'grey', or 'dark'. Var., Floyd.

LOCKWOOD (Old English) 'of the deep forest'.

LORCAN (Irish–Latin) 'bay tree'. Dim., Lanty, Larry.

LORIMER (Latin) 'lover of horses'. Var., Larimer, Larimor, Lorrimor.

LOUIS see LEWIS.

LOVEL (Anglo-Norman) 'the wolf' or 'beloved'. Var., Lovel, Lovell.

LUCIAN (Latin Pron: Loosian) 'light'. Var. and dim., Luce, Luke, Lukey, Lucins.

LUDOVIC, LODOWICK see LEWIS.

LUKE (Latin) 'of or belonging to Luciana'; the name of the 3rd Evangelist.

LUTHER (Old German) 're-nowned warrior'. Var., Lothair, Lothar, Lothario.

LYDELL (Old English) 'of the open dell'.

LYLE (French) 'from the island'. Var., Lisle.

LYNDON see LINDLEY.

LYSANDER (Greek) 'liberator'. Dim., Sandy.

M

MACE see THOMAS.

MACHAN Scottish clan name sometimes used as Christian name.

MACNAIR (Gaelic) 'son of the heir'. Dim., Mac.

MADDOC (Welsh) 'fortunate'. Var., Maddox, Madox, Maddock.

MAGNUS (Latin) 'great'.

MAITLAND (Old English) 'of the plains'. Var., Matland, Mattland, Mailand.

MALACHI (Hebrew. Pron: Malaki) 'angel of Jehovah'. Var., Malachee, Malachus, Malchus.

MALCOLM (Gaelic) 'disciple of Colombe' a favourite Scottish name.

MALLORY (Latin) 'luckless'.

MALVIN (Gaelic) 'smooth brow'. Var., Melvin.

MANFRED (Old German) 'man of peace'.

MANNING (Old German) 'coat-maker; son of a good man'. Var., Maning.

MANUEL see EMMANUEL.

MARCIAN (Latin. Pron: Marsian) 'of Mars'.

MARCUS see MARK.

MARIUS (Latin) derived from the name of the God Mars.

MARK (Latin) 'belonging to Mars; a warrior'. Var. and dim., Marc, Marcel, March, Marco, Marcus, Marcy, Marek, Mars, Martin, Martyn, Marty.

MARLOW (Old English) 'of the hill by the water'.

MARNE Irish place name.

MARSDEN (Old English) 'from the marsh valley'.

MARSHALL (French) 'marshal'. Var. and dim., Marshal, Marsh.

MARSTON (Old English) 'of the farm by the water'.

MARTIN see MARK.

MARVIN see IRVIN.

MATTHEW (Hebrew) 'God's gift'. Var. and dim., Maddis, Mathias, Mat, Matt, Matty.

MAUGER (Old German) 'spear grinder'.

MAURICE (Latin) 'dark; Moorish'. Var. and dim., Morel, Morice, Morris, Maurey, Maury, Morry.

MAX dim. of Maximillian, now a name in its own right.

MAXIMILLIAN (Latin) made by the Roman Emperor Frederic from the names of the two friends he most admired, Fabius Maximus and Scipio Aemilianus.

MAYNARD (Old German) 'enduring strength'. Var., Mainard.

MEADOWS (English) 'meadows'.

MEDWIN (Old German) 'strong friend'. Dim., Winnie.

MELCHIOR (Hebrew. Pron: Melkior) 'king of light'.

MELDON (Old English) 'of the mill on the hill'.

MELVILLE (French) place name (the name of a 4th-Century Irish saint). Dim., Mel.

MELVIN see MALVIN.

MERCER (Latin. Pron: Merser) 'merchant'. Var. and dim.,

Merceer, Mercorr, Merc, Merce.

MEREDITH (Welsh) 'lord'. Var., Meridith.

MERLIN (Old English) 'hawk; falcon'. Var. and dim., Marlen, Marlin, Marlon, Merl.

MERRICK (Old German) 'work, rule'.

MERVYN (Old English) 'sea friend'. Var., Marvin.

MEWAN Cornish form of the name Mainard, Maynard.

MICHAH (Hebrew) 'who is like God?'.

MICHAEL (Hebrew) 'God-like'. Var., and dim., Mitchell, Mickey, Mike, Mitch, Mighel, Mygel, Mignel.

MILEIN (Irish) form of the Welsh Myllin, probably 'crusher'.

MILES (Old German). Perhaps linked to Old Slavonic Milu, 'merciful'. Var., Milo.

MILO see MILES.

MILTON (Old English) 'from the mill town'. Dim., Milt.

MITCHELL see MICHAEL.

MONTAGUE (Latin) 'from the pointed mountain'. Var. and dim., Montagu, Monte.

MONTGOMERY (French) 'mountain hunter'. Dim., Monte, Monty.

MORAY (Scottish) 'great'.

MORDECAI (Hebrew, Pron: Mordekī) 'worshipper of Marduk' (God of Babylon).

MORFORD English place name.

MORGAN (Celtic) 'from the sea', or 'sea-white'.

MORLEY (Old English) 'from the moor meadow'.

MORRIS see MAURICE.

MORTIMER A surname from Mortemer in Normandy. Dim., Mort, Mortie, Morty.

MOSES (Egyptian) meaning uncertain. Var. and dim., Mose, Moss, Moe, Moyse.

MUIR (Celtic) 'moor'.

MUNGO (Gaelic) 'amiable'.

MURDOCH (Gaelic) 'sea man'. Var., Murdock, Murtagh.

MURRAY (Celtic) 'sailor'.

MYLOR (Celtic) 'prince'. Var., Melar, Milore, contraction of the Latin name Melorins.

MYRON (Greek) 'fragrant'.

N

NAHUM (Hebrew. Pron: Nayum) 'consoling'.

NALDO (Old German) 'power'.

NATHANIEL, NATHAN (Hebrew) 'God has given'. Var. and dim., Nathan, Nathanael, Nat, Nate, Natie, Natty.

NAUNTON surname sometimes used as Christian name.

NAYLOR (Old English) 'a sail-maker'. Var., Nalor, Nallor, Naylur.

NAZARIUS (Latin) 'the aloof'. Var., Nazar.

NEAL (Irish) 'champion'. Var., Neale, Neil, Nealey, Nial.

NED see **EDMUND, EDWARD.**

NEHEMIAH (Hebrew) 'consolation of God'.

NELSON (Celtic) 'Son of Neal'. Var., Neilson.

NERGAL (Babylonian) name of the God who ruled over the first day of the week.

NESTOR (Greek) 'venerable wisdom'. Var. and dim., Nessim, Nessie.

NEVILLE (Latin) Originally a Norman surname from Neuville or Neville in Normandy. Var., Nevil, Nevell.

NEVLIN (Celtic) 'sailor'.

NEWTON (Old English) literally 'from the new town'.

NIAM (Irish) probably 'champion'.

NICHOLAS (Greek) 'victory of the people'. Var. and dim., Nichol, Nicholl, Nicolas, Niles, Clause, Colin, Colley, Klaus, Nick, Nicky.

NICODEMUS (Greek) 'the people's conqueror'. Dim., Nick, Nicky.

NIGEL, NIAL (Irish) 'champion'.

NOAH (Hebrew) 'longlived'.

NOEL (Latin) 'Christmas'. Var., Newel, Newell, Noclle, Nils.

NOLAN (Irish) 'noble, famous'.

NOLL see **OLIVER.**

NORBERT (Old German) 'sea brightness'. Dim., Bert.

NORMAN (Old German) 'man from the North', or 'of Normandy'. Var. and dim., Normand, Norris, Norm, Normie.

NORRIS (Latin) 'dark'.

NORTON (Old English) 'From the north place'. Dim., Ned, Norty.

NORVAL (Old French) 'northern valley'. Var., Norvil, Norvol.

NORVIN (Old German) 'a man from the North'. Var., Norvan, Norven, Norvun.

NORWARD (Old German) 'the guard at the Northern gate'. Var., Norword.

O

OAKLEY (Old English) 'from the oak tree meadow'.

OBADIAH (Hebrew) 'servant of God'. Dim., Obe.

OBAN (Latin) 'citizen'.

OCTAVIUS (Latin) 'the eighth'.

ODELL (Old German) 'wealthy man'. Var., Odin, Odo.

OGDEN (Old English) 'from the oak valley'.

OLAF (Scandinavian) 'peace' or 'reminder'. Var., Olin.

OLIN see OLAF.

OLIVER (Latin) 'olive tree' or 'peace'. Var. and dim., Oliver, Ollie, Olvan, Noll, Nolly.

OLNEY (Old English) 'from the town of Olney'. Var., Olnay, Olnee, Ointon.

OLVAN see OLIVER.

OMAR (Arabic) 'he loves the sea; ship-maker'. Var., Omarr, Omer, Omor.

OREN (Hebrew) 'pine'. Var., Orin, Orrin.

ORION (Latin) 'giant'.

ORLANDO Italian form of Roland.

ORMOND (Old German) 'ship man'. Var., Orman, Ormand.

ORSON (Latin) 'bear'. Var., Orsini, Orsino (little bear).

ORVILLE (French) 'place name'. Var. and dim., Orvil, Orvie, Orral.

OSBERT (Old English) 'aged-bright'. Dim., Bert, Bertie, Berty, Oz, Ozzie.

OSBORN (Old English) 'a good man'. Var. and dim., Osborne, Osbourne, Ozzie.

OSCAR (Old English) 'divine spear'. Dim., Os, Ozzie.

OSMUND (Old German) 'he is protected by God'. Var. and dim., Osmand, Osmen, Osmund, Os, Osmo, Ozmo.

OSRIC (Old German) 'divine power'. Var. and dim., Osrack, Osrick, Osrock, Ossie, Rick, Rock.

OSWALD (Old English) 'divine power'. Dim., Os, Oz.

OSWIN (Old English) 'a good friend'.

OTIS (Greek) 'keen eared'.

OTTO (Old German) 'rich'.

OTTWAY (Old German) 'lucky warrior'. Var. and dim., Atway, Otway, Otweigh, Otto.

OVID (Latin) name of the Roman romantic poet.

OWEN (Celtic) 'young warrior'. Var., Owain.

P

PADDY see PATRICK.

PADARN (Irish) 'fatherly'.

PALMER (Latin) 'the palm-bearer' or 'pilgrim'.

PARK (Old English) 'of the park'. Var., Parke.

PARNELL see PETER.

PARRY (Welsh) 'Son of Harry'.

PASCAL (Hebrew) 'child of Passover'. Var., Pascalas, Pascalis, Pasco.

PASCOE (Mediaeval English) 'Easter'. Var., Pask.

PATRICK (Latin) 'noble; patrician'. Var. and dim., Padraic, Patric, Peyton, Paddy, Pat, Patsy, Patty, Rick.

PAUL (Latin) 'little'. Var. and dim., Paley, Paulie.

PAXTON (Old German) 'from

afar; a traveller'. Var., Packston, Packton, Paxon.

PEARCE, PIERCE see **PETER.**

PEDRO see **PETER.**

PEMBROKE (Celtic) 'from the headland'.

PERCIVAL (French) 'valley-piercer'. Var. and dim., Perceval, Purcell, Perce, Percy.

PERCY (French) surname from Perci the village near St. Lô in Normandy.

PEREGRINE (Latin) 'strange traveller – pilgrim'. Dim., Perry.

PERRY (Old English) 'pear tree'. Dim., Perr.

PETER (Greek) 'rock; stone'. Var. and dim., Parnell, Pearce, Pedro, Pernell, Perrin, Petrie, Pierce, Pierre, Pietro, Pete, Petey, Petie.

PETRONIUS (Latin) 'man of stubborn disposition'. Var. and dim., Petronias, Petronis, Petronus, Pete.

PHELIM (Irish. Pron: Felim) 'the ever good'.

PHILEMON (Greek) 'the kiss'. Var. and dim., Filemon, Filemel, Philemol, Phil.

PHILIP (Greek) 'lover of horses'. Var. and dim., Phelps, Phillip, Flip, Phil.

PHINEAS (Egyptian. Pron: Fineeas) 'black'.

PIERRE see **PETER.**

PIERS (Greek) 'stone'. French variation of Peter, introduced in England by the Normans.

PIRAN Cornish version of the name Kieran 'dark'. Var., Pyran.

PLATO (Latin) 'teacher of mankind'. Var., Platas, Platus, Platto, Plattu, Platon.

PORTER (Latin) 'doorkeeper' or 'gatekeeper'.

POWELL (Celtic) 'alert'.

PRENTICE (Latin) 'learner; apprentice'. Var., Prentiss.

PRESTON (Old English) 'of the priest's place'.

PRIAM (Greek) The legendary king of Troy at the time of its capture by the Greeks.

PRINCE (Latin) 'prince'.

PROCTOR (Latin) 'leader'. Var., Procter, Precto.

PROSPER (Latin) 'always blessed'. Var. and dim., Pros, Prosperus, Prosporious, Pruspas.

PROTEUS (Latin. Pron: Proteus) 'changing'. Var., Protas, Proterius, Protes.

PROTHERO (Welsh) 'the red'.

Q

QUENTIN (Latin) 'fifth'. Var. and dim., Quintin, Quent.

QUESTIN variation of Quentin.

QUILLON (Latin) 'sword hilt'. Dim., Quill, Quillion.

QUINBY (Scandinavian) 'born of woman'.

QUINCY (French) Place name.

QUINN (Irish) 'counsel'.

QUINTUS (Latin) 'the fifth'.

R

RAB see **ROBERT**.

RADCLIFFE (Old English) 'from the red cliff'.

RALEIGH (Old English) 'of the hunting lodge'. Var., Ralaigh, Ralleigh, Ralli.

RALPH (Old Norse - Old English) 'wolf counsel'.

RAMIAH (Hebrew) 'praise the Lord'. Var., Ramah.

RAMON see **RAYMOND**.

RAMSEY (Old German) 'from Ram's island'.

RANDALL see **RANDOLPH**.

RANDOLPH (Old English) 'shield-wolf'. Var. and dim., Ralph, Randal, Randall, Rolf, Rolfe, Rolph, Randy, Rand.

RAOUL (Pron: Rowl) The French form of Ralph.

RAPHAEL (Hebrew. Pron: Rafayl) 'God has healed'. Var. and dim., Rafael, Raffaello, Raff.

RAWDON (Old German) 'from the deer hill'. Var., Rawdan, Rawden, Rawdin.

RAY usually a dim. of Raymond, sometimes used as an independent name.

RAYBURN (Old English) 'of the flowered fields'. Var., Raybourne, Raybin.

RAYMOND (Old German) 'wise protection'. Var. and dim., Ramon, Raymund, Ray.

RAYNER (Old German) 'mighty folk'.

REDMOND (Old German) 'adviser; protector'.

REDVERS surname sometimes used as a Christian name.

REGINALD (Old English–German) 'mighty powerful'. Var. and dim., Regnold, Reinhold, Reynold, Ronald, Reg, Reggie, Ron, Ronnie, Ronny.

REMUS (Latin) 'fair'.

REUBEN (Hebrew: Pron: Rooben) 'behold a son!'. Var. and dim., Ruben, Rube, Ruby.

REX (Latin) 'king'.

REYNAUD either from the French 'fox' or German 'counsel army'.

RHYS (Welsh. Pron: Reece) meaning uncertain. It gave rise to the surnames Reece, Rice, Price and Preece.

RHAIN (Welsh) 'Lance'.

RHIDIAN (Welsh) 'dwells by the ford'.

RICHARD (Old German) 'stern ruler'. Var. and dim., Ricardo, Dick, Dicky, Rick, Ricky, Ritchie.

RICHMOND (Old German) 'powerful protector'.

RICKI dim. of Richard sometimes used as a name in its own right.

RIOCH (Irish) probably from Breton 'warrior'. Dim. Riok, Rio.

ROBERT (Old English–German) 'bright fame'. Var. and dim., Rab, Robard, Rob, Hob, Dob, Nob, Nobby, Rupert.

ROBIN dim. of Robert became a name in its own right, possibly because of the bird.

RODERICK (Old German) 'fame, rule'. Var., Rhoderick.

RODNEY (Old English) 'reed, island'.

ROGER (Old English–German) 'famed spear'.

ROLAND (Old German) 'famous land'.

ROLF (Old German) 'famed wolf'.

RONAN (Scottish) 'seal'.

ROMAN (Latin) 'citizen of Rome'.

ROMILLY (Latin) place name in England.

ROMMULUS (Latin) 'citizen of Rome'. Var., Romulus.

ROMNEY (Old English) 'of the town of Romney'.

RONALD, RANALD Scottish version of Reynold or Reginald.

ROQUE (Latin) 'valiant soldier'. Var. and dim., Rochus, Rock, Rocky.

RORY (Celtic) 'ruddy; red-haired'. Var., Rorie, Rorry.

ROSCOE (Old German) 'from the deer forest'. Dim., Ros, Roz.

ROSS (Old German) 'horse'.

ROSWELL (Old German) mighty steed'. Dim., Ros, Roz.

ROWAN (Scandinavian) 'mountain ash'.

ROY (Gaelic) 'red-haired'.

ROYCE (French) 'son of the king'. Var. and dim., Roice, Roi, Roy.

ROYDEN (Old English) 'from the flowered valley'.

ROYSTON (English) place name possibly 'royal town'.

RUDOLPH (Old German) 'famed wolf'. Var. and dim., Rollin, Rudolf, Dolph, Rolfe, Rollo, Ralph, Rudy, Odulf.

RUFUS (Latin) 'red-haired'. Var. and dim., Griffin, Griffith, Griff, Rufe.

RUNDEL surname sometimes used as a Christian name.

RUPERT see **ROBERT**.

RUSSELL a surname derived from the nickname Russell or Rouselle, a dim. of French roux 'red'.

RUSTICUS (Latin. Pron: Rustikus) 'from the country'. Var. and dim., Rustice, Rusty.

RUTHERFORD (Old English) 'from the cattle ford'.

S

SABER (Old German. Pron: Sayber) 'man of the sword'. Var., Sabir.

SACHEVERELL (Old French. Pron: Sasheverell) meaning uncertain, may have been Norman nickname 'sans cheverel' 'without a jacket'.

SAIRE (Old German–English) 'victory of the people'. Var., Sair, Sayre, Saer.

SALATHIEL (Babylonian) 'God is my . . . .' (The rest is unknown.)

SALISBURY (Old English) 'from the guarded palace'. Var., Salisbarry.

SALVADOR (Latin) 'of the Savior'. Dim., Sal.

SALVIN (Latin) 'saviour'.

SAMSON (Hebrew) 'child of the sun'. Var. and dim., Sampson, Simpson, Simson, Sam, Sammy, Sim.

SAMUEL (Hebrew) 'name of God'. Dim., Sam, Sammy.

SANDERS (Greek) 'son of Alexander'. Var., Saunders. See also **ALEXANDER**.

SANDOR (Hungarian) 'helper of men'.

SANDY see **SANFORD**.

SANFORD (Old English) 'sandy crossing'. Var. and dim., Sanferd, Sanfourd, Sanfo, Sandy.

SARID (Hebrew) 'one of the survivors'. Var., Sarad.

SAUL (Hebrew) 'longed for'. Welsh variation Sawl.

SAXON (Old German) 'from a Saxon town'. Var., Saxen.

SCEVO (Hebrew) 'a left-handed son'. Var., Scevor, Scevour, Scever.

SCOTT (Latin) 'a Scotsman'. Dim., Scot, Scottie, Scotty.

SEABROOKE (Old English) 'from a brook by the sea'. Var., Seabrook.

SEADON (Old English) 'of the field near the sea'. Var., Seaden, Seaddon.

SEAMUS (Pron: Shaymus). Irish form of **JAMES**. Var., Shamus, Shemus.

SEAN, SHAWN (Pron: Shawn) see **JOHN**.

SEANCHAN (Irish. Pron: Shanahan) old spelling of John.

SEBASTIAN (Greek) 'respected; reverenced'.

SEDGEWICK (Old English) 'from the village of victory'. Var., Sedgewake, Sedgewinn.

SEFTON (Old English) 'place name'. Var., Seften, Sefton.

SEGAL (Old English) literally 'seagull'.

SELBY (Old German) 'from the manor farm'. Var., Shelby.

SELDON (Old English) 'from the new valley'. Var., Seldan, Selden, Seldun.

SELIG see **ZELIG**.

SELWYN (Old English) 'house-friend'.

SELYF Irish contraction of Solomon.

SEPTIMUS (Latin) 'seventh'.

SERGIUS (Latin) 'consul'. Var. and dim., Sergias, Serge, Sergei, Sergu.

SERLE (Old English–German) 'armour'. Var., Searle.

SERNIN (Irish) contraction of Saturnius.

SETH (Hebrew) 'compensation'.

SEVERIN (Old English) 'of the Severn River'. Var., Severen, Severinus.

SEWARD (Old English) 'defender of the coast'.

SEWELL (Old German) 'victorious on the sea'. Var., Sewel, Sewoll, Sewole.

SEYMOUR (Old English) 'from the sea moor'. Var., and dim., Seymor, Sy.

SHANE see **JOHN**.

SHANNON Irish place name.

SHAW (Old English) 'from the grove'.

SHELDON (Old English) 'from the hill-ledge'. Var. and dim., Shelton, Shel, Shell, Shelly.

SHELLEY (Old English) 'from the ledge' Dim., Shel, Shell.

SHEPLEY (Old English) 'of the sheep meadow'. Var. and dim., Sheply, Shep.

SHERARD (Old English) 'a brave soldier'. Var. and dim., Shererd, Sherourd, Sherurd, Sherar, Sherr.

SHERIDAN (Celtic) 'wild man; savage'. Var. and dim., Sheriden, Sherry.

SHERLOCK (Old English) 'a fair-haired son'. Var., Sherlocke, Sherrlock.

SHERWOOD (Old English) 'bright forest'.

SHOLTO (Irish) 'sower'.

SIDDON (Hebrew) 'fisherman'. Var. and dim., Sidonius, Sidon, Sidoon, Sid, Sydney.

SIDNEY (French) 'a follower of St. Denis'. Var. and dim., Sydney, Sid, Syd.

SIEGFRID (Old German. Pron: Seegfreed) 'victorious peace.' Var., Sierfried.

SIGMUND (Old German) 'victorious protector'.

SILAS (Latin) Probably a shortening of Silvanus, the God of trees. Var. and dim., Silvan, Silvanus, Silvester, Sylvan, Sylvester, Silvins, Si.

SILLAN Irish contraction of Sylvanus.

SILOAM (Hebrew) 'he is sent forth'. Var. and dim., Siloum, Siloa.

SILVIUS (Latin) Shakespeare's version of Silvanus see **SILAS**.

SIMEON (Hebrew) 'hearkening – little hyena'.

SIMON (Hebrew) 'snub nosed'.

SIMPSON see **SAMSON**.

SINCLAIR (Latin) 'saintly; shining light'.

SION (Hebrew) 'exalted'.

SIRAN Irish contraction of Sigiranus (Latin).

SIWARD (Old English) 'victory protection'.

SLOAN (Celtic) 'warrior'.

SOCRATES (Greek. Pron: Sokrateez) 'teacher'.

SOL (Latin) 'sun'.

SOLOMON (Hebrew) 'little man of peace'. Dim., Sol, Solly.

SOMERSET English county name the most famous bearer being Somerset Maugham the novelist. Dim., Somer.

SOTER (Latin) The name of a 1st-century Pope who was martyred.

SPENCER (French) 'storekeeper'. 'dispenser of provisions'. Var. and dim., Spenser, Spence.

STACY (Latin. Pron: Staysi) 'stable comrade'. Var., Stacey.

STAFFORD (Old English) 'of the landing ford'. Var., Staffard, Staford.

STANDISH (Old English) 'of the rocky valley'. Var., Standice, Standush.

STANFORD (Old English) 'of the stony crossing'.

STANHOPPE (Old English. Pron: Stanop) 'from the stony vale'. Var., Stanhope, Stanhup.

STANISLAS (Slavonic) 'camp; glory'. The name of two Persian saints.

STANLEY surname derived from a place name. Var. and dim., Stanleigh, Stan, Lee.

STANTON (Old English) 'from the stony place'. Var., Stantan, Stantun.

STANWIN (Old English) 'a friend of nature'. Var., Stanwinn, Stonwin.

STEPHEN (Greek) 'crown; garland'. Var. and dim., Stefan, Steffen, Steven, Steve, Stevie.

STERLING (Old German) 'good value; honest; genuine'. Var., Stirling.

STEWART (Old English) 'keeper of the estate'. Var. and dim., Steward, Stuart, Stew, Stu.

STILLWELL (Old English) 'from the quiet spring'. Var., Stilwell, Stilwol.

STODDARD (Old English) 'keeper of horses'.

STRATFORD English place name.

STUART see STEWART.

SUMNER (Latin) 'one who summons and calls'.

SWITHIN (Old English) 'strong'. Var., Swithun.

SYLVESTER (Latin. Pron: Silvester) 'growing in a wood'.

T

TABBER (Arabic) 'little drummer'. Var., Taber.

TAIT (Scandinavian) 'of great joy'. Var., Taite.

TALBOT (Old English) 'woodcutter'. Var., Tallbot, Tallbott.

TAM, TAMMANY, TOMAS see **THOMAS.**

TAMLAN (Scottish) 'twin'. Var., Tamlane.

TANCRED (Old German) 'thoughtful counsel'.

TARQUIN (Latin. Pron: Tarkwin) The name of two Roman Emperors. Var., Tarkin.

TARRSUS (Hebrew) 'from the city of Tarrsus'. Var., Tarsus, Tarsuss.

TATE (Old German) 'cheerful'.

TAUBE (English) 'brown-tawny'.

TAURION the name of an early Macedonian saint and martyr.

TAVIS (Celtic) 'son of David'.

TEAGUE (Irish) 'poet'. Var., Teage, Tadleigh, Teighe.

TEARLE (Old English) 'a serious soul'. Var., Teerell, Tierell, Terle.

TED, TEDDY see **THEODORE.**

TEILLO (Latin) 'bright pupil'. Var., Teilo.

TELEN 6th-century Irish saint.

TERENCE (Latin) meaning uncertain. Var. and dim., Terrence, Torrance, Terry.

TERRILL (Old German) 'belonging to Thorr; martial'.

TERTIUS (Latin. Pron: Tershius) 'third son'.

THADDEUS (Hebrew) 'praise to God'. Dim., Tad, Thad.

THALAS (Latin) 'benevolent'. Dim., Thalaseuis, Thalus.

THANE (Scottish) 'king'.

THATCHER (Old English) 'a mender of roofs'. Var., Thacher, Thackeray, Thaxter.

THAYER (Old German) 'of the nation's army'.

THEOBALD see **TYBALT.**

THEODORE (Greek) 'gift of God'. Var. and dim., Feodor, Feodore, Tudor, Dore, Tad, Ted, Teddie, Teddy, Theo, Theodoric.

THERNOT (Old Irish) meaning uncertain.

THERRON (Greek) 'the hunter'. Var., Theron.

THEYDON (English) place name.

THOMAS (Aramaic) 'the twin'. Var. and dim., Tomas, Tammany, Tam, Tammy, Thom, Tom, Tommy, Mace.

THORLEY (Old English) 'of the grounds of Thorr'. Var., Thorlay, Thorlie.

THORNTON (Old English) 'from the thorny place'.

THURSTON (Scandinavian) 'Thor's jewel or stone'.

TIAN (Irish. Pron: Teean) meaning uncertain.

TIBERIUS (Latin) 'The Roman River'. Dim., Tib.

TIERNAN (Celtic) 'kingly'. Var., Tierney, Tiernay.

TIMOTHY (Greek) 'honouring God'. Dim., Tim, Timmie.

TITUS (Latin–Greek. Pron: Titus) 'honoured'. Var. and dim., Tito.

TOBIAS (Hebrew) 'God's goodness'. Var. and dim., Tobin, Tobit, Tobe, Toby.

TOM, TOMMY see **THOMAS**.

TONY see **ANTHONY**.

TORQUIL (Scandinavian. Pron: Torkwil) 'Thor's cauldron'. Var., Torkail.

TORRANCE see **TERENCE**.

TRADER surname sometimes used as Christian name.

TRAHERN (Celtic. Pron: Trahern) 'powerful leader'. Var., Trahurn.

TRAVERS (Latin) 'from the crossroad'. Var., Travis.

TRELAWN Irish place name.

TREMAIN (Old English) 'of the ruins'. Var., Tremahn, Tremaynne.

TRENT (Latin) 'swift'.

TREVORR (Celtic) 'careful traveller'. Var., Trevarr, Treverr, Trevor.

TRISTAN (Latin) 'sorrowful' tumultuous'. Dim., Tris, Tristram.

TROILUS (Greek. Pron: Troylus) the hero of Shakespeare's play *Troilus and Cressida.*

TROY dim., of Troilus.

TRUMAN (Old English) 'a faithful man'.

TUDOR (Welsh) 'a gift of the Lord'. Var., Tuddor.

TYBALT (Old English. Pron: Tibalt) 'leader of people.' Var. and dim., Theobald, Thibaut, Tybald.

TYLER (Old English) 'maker of tiles or bricks'. Var. and dim., Taylor, Ty.

TYRONE (Celtic. Pron: Tirone) of uncertain meaning. Dim., Ty.

TYSON (Pron: Tison) 'son of the German'. Dim., Sonny, Ty.

U

ULAND (Old German. Pron: Yuland) 'from a noble land'. Var., Ulund, Ulland, Ullund.

ULRIC, ULRICH (Pron: Ulrick) see **ALARIC**.

ULTANN (Welsh) 'saintly'. Var., Ultan, Ultun.

ULYSSES (Pron: Yuliseez) The Latin name for the Greek hero Odysseus.

V

VAL (Old German) 'might; power'. Also dim., of any name beginning with Val.

VALENTINE (Latin) 'healthy; strong; valorous'. Var., Valente, Valiant.

VALERIAN (Latin. Pron: Valeerian) meaning uncertain. The name of a famous Roman people.

VALMOND (Germanic) 'power-protection'.

VANBRUGH (Pron: Vanbru). Christian name taken from the name of a famous English family.

VANCE (Dutch) 'the son of Vandyke', or 'the son of Vaness'. Var., Van.

VANDYKE (Dutch) 'keeper of the dyke'. Dim., Van.

VARIAN (Latin. Pron: Vairian) 'clever; capricious'. Var., Varien, Varion, Varrian.

VARRIUS (Latin) possibly 'stranger'.

VAUGHAN (Celtic. Pron: Vawn) 'the small'. Var., Vaughn.

VERE (French) place name, Ver in Normandy.

VERNON (French) a place name often used in France. Var., Vern, Verne.

VICTOR (Latin) 'the conqueror'. Var. and dim., Victoir, Vittorio, Vic, Vick.

VIGOR (Celtic. Pron: Veegor) 'vigor'.

VINCENT (Latin) 'the conqueror'. Dim., Vin, Vince, Vinnie, Vinny.

VINSON (Old English) 'son of Vinn', thus, 'the conqueror's son'.

VIRGIL (Latin. Pron. Verjill) 'strong; flourishing'. Var. and dim., Vergil, Virg, Virgie, Virgy.

VIVIAN (Latin) 'lively'.

VOLNEY (Old German) 'most popular'. Var. and dim., Volnay, Volny, Olney.

VYCHAN (Welsh) 'little'.

W

WADE (Old English) 'mover; wanderer'.

WALCOTT (Old English) 'cottage dweller'.

WALDEMAR (Old English) 'power rule'. Dim., Waldo.

WALKER (Old English) 'forest walker'.

WALLACE Scottish surname used as a Christian name after the great leader of Scottish resistance, Sir William Wallace, Var. and dim., Wallis, Walsh, Wallie, Wally.

WALTER (Old German) 'ruler of the people'. Var. and dim., Walters, Wallie, Wally, Wait.

WARD (Old English) 'watchman; guardian'. Var., Word.

WARING (Old English) 'the cautious soul'. Var. and dim., Warring, Warrin.

WARNER (Old German) 'protecting warrior'. Var., Werner.

WARREN From old German Varin, a folk name.

WARRICK (Old German) 'strong ruler'. Var., Aurick, Vareck, Varick, Warwick.

WARTTON (Old English) 'of the town by the wall'. Var., Warton, Wartten.

WAYLAND The Saxon Smith-God.

WAYNE (Old German) 'wagon-maker'. Var., Waine, Wain.

WEBSTER (Old English) 'weaver'. Dim., Web, Webb.

WELBY (Scandinavian) 'from the farm by the spring'.

WELDON (Old German) 'from a hill near the well'.

WENDELL (Old German) 'wanderer'. Var., Wendel.

WENSLEY maybe English form of German Wenzel, 'crown glory'.

WESCOTT (Old German) 'dwells at west cottage'. Dim., Wes.

WESLEY (Old English) 'from the west meadow'. Var. and dim., Westley, Wes.

WEYMAN surname sometimes used as a Christian name, could be 'cow herd'.

WILFRED (Old English) 'will-peace'. Var. and dim., Wilfrid, Fred, Freddie.

WILL, WILLY see **WILLIAM.**

WILLIAM (Old German) 'will-helmet'. Var. and dim., Wilhelm, Willet, Willis, Bill, Billie, Billy, Will, Willy.

WILLOUGHBY (English) place name.

WINSLOW (Old German) 'from the friendly hill'. Dim., Win.

WILSON (Old German) 'son of William'. Dim., Wil.

WINSTON Name taken from a hamlet near Cirencester. Var. and dim., Winton, Win.

WOLFE (Old German) 'a wolf'. Var., Wolf.

WOLFRAM (Old German) 'respected; feared'.

WOODLEY (Old English) 'from the wooded meadow'. Dim., Woodie, Woody.

WOODROW (Old English) 'from the hedgerow in the wood'. Dim., Woodie, Woody.

WYATT (French) 'a guide'.

WYMOND Cornish place name used by the famous family of Carew.

WYNSTAN (Old English) 'battle stone'. Var., Wistan.

X

XAVIER (Arabic. Pron: Zayvier) 'bright'. Var., Javier.

XENOS (Greek. Pron: Zenoss) 'stronger'.

XERXES (Persian. Pron: Zerkseez) 'king'.

XYSTUS (Latin) 'sixth'.

Y

YATES (Old English) 'the gate dweller or protector'.

YESTIN Welsh form of Justin.

YONTY Welsh dim. of John.

YORICK Shakespeare's phonetic spelling of Yorg, the Danish form of George.

YORK (Latin) 'sacred tree'. Var., Yorick, Yorke.

YVES (Scandinavian. Pron: Eev) 'an archer'. Var., Ives, Yvon.

Z

ZACHARIAH (Hebrew. Pron: Zakarīa) 'God has remembered'. Var. and dim., Zacharias, Zach, Zack, Zakes.

ZACHARY (English dim. of Zachariah) sometimes used as a name in its own right.

ZADOC (Hebrew) 'just'. Var., Zadok.

ZANE see **JOHN**.

ZARACK possibly English corruption of Hebrew 'remembrance'.

ZAVER English pronunciation of the name of the French saint Francois.

ZEBEDEE (Hebrew) meaning uncertain. The father of two of the apostles.

ZEBULON (Hebrew. Pron: Zebyulon) 'dwelling place'. Dim., Lon, Lonny, Zeb.

ZEKE see **EZEKIEL**.

ZELIG (Old German) 'blessed'. Var., Selig.

ZENNOR Cornish place name.

ZENON (Greek) from Zeus.

HEALTH AND SELF-HELP BOOKS NOW AVAILABLE IN GRANADA PAPERBACKS

W H Bates
Better Eyesight Without Glasses   £1.95 ☐

Christine Beels
The Childbirth Book   £1.95 ☐

Desmonde Dunne
Yoga Made Easy   £1.50 ☐

Laurence E Morehouse & Leonard Gross
Total Fitness   £1.25 ☐
Maximum Performance   95p ☐

Constance Mellor
Guide to Natural Health   £1.25 ☐
Natural Remedies for Common Ailments   £1.95 ☐

Sonya Richmond
Yoga and Your Health   £1.25 ☐

Phyllis Speight
Homoeopathy   £1.50 ☐

Ronald Gatty PhD
The Body Clock Diet   £1.50 ☐

Kenneth Lysons
How to Cope with Hearing Loss   95p ☐

Drs Andrew & Penny Stanway
The Breast   £1.95 ☐

All these books are available at your local bookshop or newsagent, and can be ordered direct from the publisher.

To order direct from the publisher just tick the titles you want and fill in the form below:

Name _____

Address _____

_____

Send to:
Granada Cash Sales
PO Box 11, Falmouth, Cornwall TR10 9EN

Please enclose remittance to the value of the cover price plus:

UK 45p for the first book, 20p for the second book plus 14p per copy for each additional book ordered to a maximum charge of £1.63.

BFPO and Eire 45p for the first book, 20p for the second book plus 14p per copy for the next 7 books, thereafter 8p per book.

Overseas 75p for the first book and 21p for each additional book.

Granada Publishing reserve the right to show new retail prices on covers, which may differ from those previously advertised in the text or elsewhere.